S0-BXX-967

TEN DECADES OF PRAISE

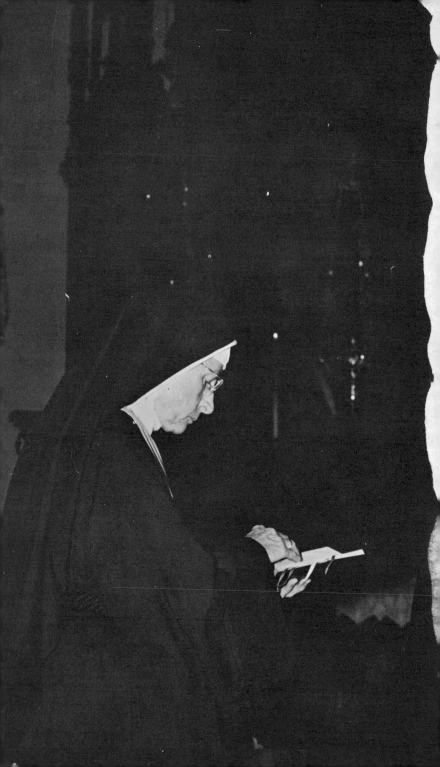

TEN DECADES OF PRAISE

The Story of the Community of Saint Mary During its First Century : 1865 to 1965

BY SISTER MARY HILARY, CSM

DeKoven Foundation · Racine, Wisconsin

SUSAN LAWRENCE EMLEY

$1.65
Copyright 1965
Paperback edition 1967
The DeKoven Foundation for Church Work
Racine, Wisconsin

To the glory of God
and in honor of Blessed Mary,
whose hidden life of faith and love
they seek to share,
the Sisters of Saint Mary
offer this chronicle
of mysteries joyful and sorrowful,
confident that the glorious mysteries
are yet to be

Preface

IN SETTING OUT to publish the centennial story of the Community of Saint Mary, the Sisters elected to tell the story themselves, candidly and objectively, omitting nothing essential to the century's total achievement; they chose to relate this story to relevant conditions and events in Church life generally; and they decided to present selected passages from the primary sources used, hoping thereby to give this popular account something of the integrity and conviction usually found only in scholarly works.

Insofar as these techniques have produced a believable and readable narrative, the credit is largely due, first, to the history-conscious Sisters through the years who have carefully assembled and deposited in the Community archives full accounts of significant events; and second, to the Associates and friends in Chicago, Memphis and New York whose interest and generosity opened many doors. For inaccuracies and inadequacies the author alone is responsible and must one day account to the Sisters now sleeping in nameless graves whose triumphs have taught her much and whose failures she is unworthy to recount.

Contents

CHAPTER ONE

The Work of God

FIVE MINUTES BEFORE TWELVE the warning bell rings. The kitchen Sister slips out of a blue apron and makes a final check of the refectory tables; the guest mistress pauses in the cloister with a visiting Associate, helping her mark the proper pages in her breviary; a Novice snatches the convent cat and ejects him from the sacristy.

Up the hill from the altar-bread bakery, down the hill from the laundry, in from the garden, out of the Convent offices, down the stairs from the sewing room, come Sisters of Saint Mary in their soaring starched headpieces. Within a few minutes they have entered the Chapel and are kneeling in choir, in places assigned by rank. The Office bell rings, the Superior announces the intention for which they are offering this act of worship—for Christian education at Prime and successively for the visible unity of the Church, the conversion of sinners, for the sick, the poor, for benefactors, associates and families—and together they chant the

3

hymn and the psalms which, with a brief scripture lesson, the Lord's Prayer and a collect, make up the mid-day Little Hours.

The Divine Office is recited carefully, with a direct and quiet simplicity that worldlings, accustomed to over-assertion, find disconcerting. Critics of monasticism have called it dreary psalm-droning, but to the Benedictine-oriented Community of Saint Mary, the Divine Office is the very heart of the life of the gospel counsels of perfection. The Sisters have set out to love a sinful and sordid world with the saving love of Christ. Only because of him, and through him, are they able to do this. Thus they turn again and again to the drama of redemption. Each hour of worship celebrates the *Israel out of Egypt* event which prefigured and pointed toward Christ's deliverance of mankind from sin's bondage. At the longer Offices of Lauds and Vespers the choir chants the gospel canticles heralding the Saviour: Our Lady's *Magnificat* at Vespers and Zacharias's *Benedictus* at Lauds.

The Divine Office is seen, then, as the pageant of salvation continuously offered in praise of God on behalf of the Church, in intercession for all men. Its setting varies kaleido-scopically with the seasons of the liturgical year, sorrowful and stark in the nights before Good Friday, bursting forth on Easter with bells, lights and flowers to herald Christ's victory over sin and death. When she is in choir, a Sister of Saint Mary speaks as the voice of Christ in his body the Church. She goes forth from the great redemption drama to live its message before an unbelieving world, to put love where there is no love, as St. John of the Cross once said.

Whenever the Catholic Church has been most truly and fully Christ-in-the-world, she has been faithful to this *Opus*

Dei, the regular and continuous praising of God as his due, his worth-ship. At the English Reformation and its aftermath, when many tools of devotion were discarded or neglected, this was retained in the Prayer Book Offices of Matins and Evensong. From the Divine Office as it was recited by cathedral canons, by vicars and their flocks, by country squires and their households, it was but a step to the Offices as they were recited at Little Gidding in the seventeenth century, and another step to the revival of conventual communities in nineteenth century England.

In the United States, the barriers to resuming the *Opus Dei* seemed insurmountable. Although by 1800 despite widespread opposition and suspicion, the Anglicans had acquired bishops, the Church was still an orphaned and exiled child in a hostile Puritan and Deist environment, uncertain of its identity and cut off from its heritage. Even so, it was a parishioner of Trinity Church in New York who made the first move toward founding an indigenous community for women. So far ahead of her time was Eliza Bayley Seton that she was obliged to seek Roman Catholic sponsorship for her Daughters of Charity.

It was Mrs. Seton's rector, John Henry Hobart, who, as Bishop of New York, directed the initial phase of revival. Anglican renewal flourished until the 1830's, when it was halted by the cross-fire of the Catholic-Protestant nativist vendetta. Alarmed by increased Irish immigration, evangelical preachers and editors from 1835 to 1855 waged a campaign of vilification so perfidious that they actually succeeded in "poisoning the wells of history", as Bishop Ireland once charged. The no-popery propagandists turned to publishing alleged disclosures of the enormities of convent life,

5

producing a literary genre that has been largely disregarded by American historians. Such books as *Six Months in a Convent* by Rebecca Theresa Reed and the notorious *Awful Disclosures of the Hotel Dieu Nunnery of Montreal* by Maria Monk are credited with the widest sale of any titles published prior to *Uncle Tom's Cabin* in 1852. By such means, incalculable numbers of Americans were persuaded that nuns represented "white female slaves in this land of freedom", as the American Protective Association declared at its first meeting in Clinton, Iowa, in 1887.

Thus when Dr. William Augustus Muhlenberg set out to found the first sisterhood in the Episcopal church, he was careful to disclaim any resemblance to Roman Catholic nunneries, and appears to have initiated the venture with utmost secrecy. Only he and the sexton witnessed the brief ceremony on the Feast of All Saints, 1845, when the thirty-nine-year-old Anne Ayres knelt at the altar of the Church of the Holy Communion in Manhattan and consecrated her life to the service of Christ as a Sister of the Holy Communion. Dr. Muhlenberg envisaged no nunnery, he assured distraught parishioners, but rather an association of deaconesses such as that proposed by his friend the Rev. William Alfred Passavant, a Lutheran minister. In 1849, Pastor Theodor Fliedner, founder of the deaconess institute at Kaiserswerth, Germany, chaperoned four deaconesses from Kaiserswerth to Pittsburgh to staff Dr. Passavant's hospital, thereby founding the order in the United States. It was to this order of deaconesses that Dr. Muhlenberg always pointed when the no-nunnery alarm sounded.

Briefly stated, Dr. Muhlenberg's formula called for a woman of great force of character who would be the centre around whom the others are to rally, carrying out her directions and deriving through her, in return, supplies, protection, and all needful provision for their comfort.

This superintending sister he planned to invest with "enough control to secure efficient service, and to prevent any sudden rupture and lapses in the work." A sister's commitment was for three years and she was expected to have private means of support. If the sisters took no vows, Dr. Muhlenberg explained, then members whose zeal flagged would be free to depart, and monastic decay could never take place.

In formulating his ideal, Dr. Muhlenberg displayed all the faults of his virtues. His was a religion entirely of the heart; his revulsion upon meeting Newman at Oxford in 1843 was the natural, distrustful response of a sentimental man confronted with the hard facets, as well as the shadowed subtlety, of Newman's intellect. Dr. Muhlenberg's attitudes were largely sectarian; born into a distinguished Lutheran family in Philadelphia, he appears to have become an Anglican by chance. When St. James' Episcopal Church presented his widowed mother with a pew in part payment for a piece of real estate, she thriftily decided to use it. As a result, young William was sent to a school sponsored by Christ Church. There is a distinctively American and sectarian quality in Dr. Muhlenberg's insistence that the Sisters of his order could achieve the fruits of renunciation without renunciation. He ignored the fundamental principle of Catholic spirituality, that the first question must not be, "What can I do for God?", but rather "What will I allow God to do for me?" Christians are incapable of good works until they have learned the hard lessons of humility, a humility that involves acceptance—of the past and the achieve-

7

ments it has handed on to the present, of one's own limitations, of the disciplines required by community with widely diverse persons and opinions. Dr. Muhlenberg ignored also the fundamental psychological principle of over-determination; men seldom surrender themselves to the mundane and practical, and when they do, one is inclined to regard it as an abberation or at least a truncation of man's full humanity.

More surprising, Dr. Muhlenberg's scheme disregarded the gospel counsels. Obedience, most basic of the counsels, became indenture instead of a dynamic relationship with God protected by a rule and constitution and subject to Christian charity. Poverty was reduced to middleclass gentility, neither voluntary nor communal. Celibate chastity became a temporary expedient which, in certain cases, amounted to nothing more than the deferment of marriage.

Just as commitment fell short of total dedication, so the tools and aids traditionally provided in the conventual life were withheld. No provision was made for training or for retreats. The Divine Office was not recited, and worship was restricted to what Dr. Muhlenberg considered safely protestant and evangelical. The religious habit, a helpful though not essential sign and safeguard of consecration, was forbidden in favor of a prescribed, plain "ordinary attire of a gentlewoman." There was provided no episcopal oversight nor any corporate structure within which the Sisterhood could re-group itself when differences arose or leadership failed.

To say all this is to detract in no way from Dr. Muhlenberg's achievement. The courage required to establish a sisterhood is a measure of his pastoral concern for the sickness, homelessness and poverty all about. For several years

8

Miss Ayres and Miss Meta Brevoort taught in the Holy Communion parish school, visited the poor and nursed during the recurring cholera epidemics. In 1852 the Sisterhood was formally organized. In 1853 two or three rooms were hired in a tenement at the rear of the church, and beds set up for several incurable patients in desperate need of nursing. More than two hundred patients had been cared for in these lowly quarters when, in 1856, Mr. John Swift presented the Sisters with a house; their former rooms were then used to enlarge the infirmary and the ground floor given over to the school and dispensary.

II

About this time, perhaps in 1853, Harriet Starr Cannon came down from Bridgeport, Connecticut, and took a room in Brooklyn, where she planned to support herself by teaching music. The Sisterhood must have come to her attention in the general speculation and apprehension concerning it. She may have read the pamphlet "Thoughts on Evangelical Sisterhoods" written by Miss Ayres and published in 1853. In any event, on Ash Wednesday, February 6, 1856, Miss Cannon was received as a probationer in the Sisterhood of the Holy Communion, an event she always regarded as the beginning of her life in holy religion.

Harriet Cannon at thirty-three was singularly free of worldly ties. She had been born May 7, 1823, in Charleston, South Carolina, where her father had gone from Connecticut to establish a stock brokerage. Yellow fever took the lives of both parents when Harriet was seventeen months old. William Cannon died September 29, 1824, and Sarah Hinman Cannon died the following day. Harriet and her three-year-old sister, Catherine Ann, were left alone. According to family stories, everything the children should have inherited was stolen from them, though it is doubtful if William Cannon's brief business career could have yielded much in excess of his debts. The babies were soon rescued by Sally Cannon's brother-in-law, Captain James Allen, who arrived in his sailing packet on a trading venture and carried them off to relatives in Connecticut. Old accounts fail to mention whether or not a sailor in the crew was experienced in the care and feeding of infants. The pair somehow survived the ordeal and were handed over, doubtless with relief, to their mother's sister, Mrs. Hyde, in Bridgeport.

The Hyde home was full of children, the little orphans making seven. Of Harriet's childhood little is known. She was baptized in Connecticut and confirmed by Bishop Onderdonk on March 10, 1844, at the Church of the Redemption in New York, where she was visiting relatives. An accident deprived her of the sight of one eye when she tossed her head while her long, black hair was being combed, and the comb entered her eye. Music was her chief interest; she studied singing and learned to play the piano and the organ well enough to give music lessons to the children of friends and relatives.

In later girlhood, Harriet was described by a relative as "a great society girl and not at all religious." She enjoyed dancing. One of her youthful dancing partners became a Manhattan bank president who regaled his teen-aged daughter with tales of taking Harriet Cannon to parties. A miniature of the Cannon sisters done in 1850 or 1851 shows Harriet wearing somewhat exotic drop earrings and a cross on a chain, evidence perhaps that she was subject to warring

10

attractions. In her heart there must have been some seed of desire that would issue in consecration, for later in life she likened her young self to St. Theresa embarking from the nursery in Avila to convert the Moors.

The Bridgeport episode ended in 1851 when Catherine Cannon married John Ruggles and moved to California. The young couple planned that as soon as they were established Harriet would join them. Two years later the Hyde family moved to Milford, Connecticut. At some time between these two events, Harriet went to Brooklyn, where she taught music, and sang in the Grace Church choir. In 1855 she prepared to leave for California and paid a parting visit to one of her Hyde cousins, now married and living in Milford. About a week before Harriet's departure, they celebrated her birthday with a party. In the midst of the festivities, a telegram arrived announcing the death, after a brief illness, of Catherine Cannon Ruggles.

It was a crushing loss. No one ever took her sister's place in Harriet's affections. Forty years later she wrote to a Sister:

> I know how you miss your dear mother. No one knows that better than I do. All these years have gone by, and I can never speak of my sister without the tears coming with the words.
>
> You know, she was my all—neither father, mother, or brother. We were two, but were but one—but if God had left her with me, I should not have been here.

So it happened that in 1856 Harriet Cannon was received as a probationer by the Sisters of the Holy Communion and was set to work nursing in the little infirmary behind the Church of the Holy Communion, caring for eighteen patients, all seriously ill. At one point, the Sisters were quar-

11

antined with small-pox patients, a disease to which Sister
Harriet was immune by reason of previous illness. Dr.
Muhlenberg's daily visits provided their only communication
with the outside world. Sister Anne's description of one such
visit might well have described Sister Harriet:

> On one of these occasions, he found a young probationary
> Sister, rocking, as he lay wrapped in a blanket within her arms,
> a little boy, very ill with the loathsome disease. She was singing
> a hymn for him, and the poor child smiled as he looked up in
> her face and forgot his pain and restlessness. Dr. Muhlenberg
> came down from the ward enamored of the picture—'The very
> ideal of a Sister of Charity.'

In the following year, on the Feast of the Purification,
February 2, 1857, Harriet Cannon was received into full
membership as a United Sister of the Holy Communion. She
signed the rules and entered into an engagement to remain
for three years, a compact which was later renewed. With the
other Sisters, she looked forward to the completion of St.
Luke's Hospital on Fifth Avenue at Fifty-fourth Street. Dr.
Muhlenberg had first mentioned the hospital in a sermon
in 1846, and characteristically designated half the collection
at that service as the beginning of the hospital fund. As this
was the princely sum of $15, a vestryman felt impelled to
ask him when he expected his hospital to be built. "Never,
unless I begin," the priest replied. By the spring of 1857
the building rose, a stately monument to Dr. Muhlenberg's
dream of a hospital where the poor could be nursed and provided with the religious consolations and other comforts of a
loving home. A hospital, he thought, should be like a family,
with a father, a mother, and daughters to help nurse the
sick. The Sisters, therefore, were an integral part of the plan,

12

and when donors objected to "the Protestant nuns", Dr. Muhlenberg gave them his terms: no Sisters, no St. Luke's.

On the Feast of the Ascension, 1857, the hospital chapel was dedicated with appropriate services, but much remained to finish the wards. To speed the contractors, three Sisters and nine patients took possession on May 11, 1858, in a building not yet equipped with lights and lacking even a kitchen range.

The wards had been completed by September 29 when Sister Harriet joined her Sisters at St. Luke's. She was placed in charge of one of the wards, a room 109 feet long, containing forty beds. Two nurses helped her during the day, and one at night, but it was Sister Harriet who was present at the visits of the physician and was accountable for the carrying out of his directions. In a little pharmacy adjoining the ward she prepared each prescription as it was required. She saw to it that patients in her ward had opportunity to take part in the daily chapel services, from the gallery that opened onto the chapel from each ward.

There were immense satisfactions in the work. Her nursing skills increased steadily, and she had a sense of performing a useful service, of participating in a venture which attracted favorable attention from every quarter. Medical authorities from abroad remarked on the absence of the sights and odors peculiar to hospitals, the result of free ventilation, an abundance of clean bedding and dressings, and the constant care and attention of the Sisters. Moreover, Dr. Muhlenberg, a bachelor, transferred his residence to the Hospital in 1859, and since he took his meals with the Sisters, he now became a welcome member of their small family.

13

But the sands of human personality proved to be an unsound foundation upon which to build a growing Sisterhood. The Sisters complained of erratic and autocratic direction; Sister Anne responded with increased demands and tightened controls. She opposed their suggestion that the Sisterhood adopt the corporate organization and the traditional ways of the conventual life. Early in the winter of 1862-1863, United Sister Louisa Cooper and Probationary Sister Amelia Asten left the Hospital to avoid further discord. Sister Anne concluded that two courses of action lay before her: she must conform to the Sisters' requests or she must resign her office. She decided to resign and announced her decision to the Sisterhood. At once Dr. Muhlenberg, to the consternation of the Sisters, informed them that the Sisterhood was *ipso facto* dissolved. The work at St. Luke's Hospital was to be continued under Miss Ayres as matron, with such Sisters as chose to remain. Before the change could be made, however, Sister Anne angrily ordered Sisters Harriet and Mary off the premises and their appeal to Dr. Muhlenberg met with his refusal to interfere.

Accordingly, four Sisters left St. Luke's Hospital early in the morning of April 9, 1863—Harriet Cannon, Mary Heartt, Jane Haight and Sarah Bridge. Accompanying them was "Little Katie Hassett", a sixteen-year-old orphan suffering from the effects of what was described as "hip disease." Nursed back to health in Sister Harriet's ward, she had stayed on to help with the work and now hoped to become a Sister.

The Sisters never became reconciled to their abrupt departure from St. Luke's. Sister Harriet grieved to part without a word of farewell from people with whom she had worked for seven years. She returned the following day to attempt a reconciliation, but Sister Anne declined to see her. As time went on, Sister Harriet recalled with pleasure the hard work and jokes and fun they had had together at St. Luke's. She always ended with a lament over the estrangement from Sister Anne, "If only she could have trusted me."

The Sisters who remained at St. Luke's later divided into two groups. Those who worked at the Hospital and the social service complex on Long Island called St. Johnland became the Sisters of St. Luke and St. John. Those who worked from the Church of the Holy Communion became the reconstituted Sisters of the Holy Communion; these Sisters continued in charge of the dispensary at 328 Sixth Avenue for several years after the Sisterhood of St. Luke and St. John became defunct. The last Sister of the Holy Communion died in 1940.

After Dr. Muhlenberg's death in 1877, Sister Anne retired to St. Johnland where she wrote an account of her thirty-years' association with Dr. Muhlenberg. Her comments serve to show that the individual and the personal were never submerged in the corporate communal life. Sister Anne lived until 1896; she died of bronchitis in St. Luke's Hospital on February 9, just two months before Mother Harriet's death. Toward the end Mother Harriet went to visit her, somewhat apprehensively, not certain how she would be received. Her fears were groundless, however. Both had been certain of being wronged, but both had learned to forgive. Sister Anne received her guest with great kindness, and the two talked together calmly and quietly with no apparent rancor. At Sister Anne's funeral, Mother Harriet was among those who stood beside the grave.

15

Sister Harriet in the "plain, ordinary dress of a gentlewoman" prescribed for the Sisters of the Holy Communion.

Sister Sarah as a Sister of the Holy Communion, showing the delicacy which concealed a flinty resolve and loyalty.

Old St. Luke's Hospital, Fifth Avenue at Fifty-fourth Street, where the first five Sisters of Saint Mary worked as nurses and Sisters of the Holy Communion, under Anne Ayers.

Photographed in 1862 at the age of sixty, the Rt. Rev. Horatio Potter, Bishop of New York, was austere and erect, with set jaw indicating his dislike of cameras and all publicity.

The Rt. Rev. George Franklin Seymour, Bishop of Illinois, friend and champion of the Sisters from his days as chaplain at the House of Mercy.

CHAPTER TWO

Preparation

THE SISTERS WHO LEFT St. Luke's Hospital that April morning in 1863 dispersed to the nearby homes of relatives and friends, that they might meet frequently to discuss their future as a Sisterhood. Jane Haight, their leader at this point, consulted her former rector, the Rev. E. Folsom Baker. When a request arrived early in May for Sisters to assume management of the House of Mercy, however, Sister Jane was ill at her home in Catskill, New York, and Sister Harriet came in from South Orange to consider the matter. The prospective work sounded forbidding to her. She wrote Miss Ellen Kemble, Secretary of the Ladies' Committee, that they would be unable to decide until they had discussed the matter with Sarah Bridge's father, who was expected in New York that week. The House of Mercy had been established "for the reception and reformation of destitute women who may wish to abandon a vicious course of life," as stated in its charter, granted on February 2, 1855. In the Civil War era,

17

the care and reformation of prostitutes was not regarded as suitable employment for a lady; Mr. Bridge made it clear that his daughter would not be permitted to take part in the project.

There were other factors that deterred the Sisters. The 1862 report admitted delicately "the pecuniary prospects of the House are not bright." This meant, the Sisters learned, that $2,917 was due to Mrs. William Richmond, director, for money advanced by her; a $6,000 mortgage was outstanding; and the House owed a number of incidental debts.

Still, the Sisters were intrigued by the immense opportunity and the desperate need for this work of reclamation. Mrs. Richmond's husband, the Rev. William Richmond, had begun the work in 1854 when he was Rector of St. Michael's, Bloomingdale. After his death, Mrs. Richmond had bravely carried on the rescue program, against overwhelming odds. Immigrants flooding in from Ireland and Germany had swelled the city population to 813,699, of whom nearly half were foreign-born, obliged by poverty and sickness to find shelter in one of the festering slums, or in the shanty-towns huddling among the rocks of upper Manhattan. A city inspector's report for 1863 noted the plight of eighteen thousand persons living in underground cellars; of more than forty thousand unclaimed and vagrant children roaming the alleys and wharves; of twenty-five thousand prostitutes, most under twenty and many diseased. The Prison Association reported that few prostitutes lived beyond twenty-five, and that an estimated two thousand girls fell into prostitution every year, many of them mere children lured by promises of honest employment. Faced with this situation, Mrs. Richmond acquired an old mansion on Bloomingdale Road, now

Riverside Drive, near West Eighty-sixth Street. Luxurious in its day, the Howland mansion had deteriorated into a road house catering to the sporting crowds that used Bloomingdale Road for a Sunday driving course. Before the front door was the abandoned foundation of a tenement house, filled with stagnant water. Broken glass and trash littered the once proud old lawn, and burdock and thistle abounded.

The mansion's dingy rooms were furnished with broken furniture in untidy array. In 1860 Mrs. Richmond had fallen ill with cancer. Feeling her life slipping away, and seeing the desperate plight of helpless children on every hand, she felt driven to do what she could. Organizing and soliciting funds left her scant time for domestic details and, as her health failed, the house became chaotic.

Undeterred by all this, or by the bloody draft riots of July, the Sisters decided in mid-summer that it was their duty to undertake the management of the House of Mercy. On September 1, Sisters Jane, Harriet and Mary, with Catharine Hassett, took over operation of the House. Mrs. Richmond was not on hand to welcome them, having gone to Albany to bring back a runaway. The fifteen inmates were dressed in rags and run-down shoes, or no shoes at all. They watched with suspicion and scorn as the Sisters prepared the chapel for the brief installation service to take place that evening. There was no altar. A starch box served as lectern, a dirty surplice hung limply from a nail, torn books were scattered about and the whole forlorn scene was lit dimly by tallow dips in green bottles.

Investigation disclosed that the girls lived on a diet consisting chiefly of dry bread moistened with left-over tea or coffee. They confided to Sister Mary that every time the cook

19

burnt the broth they beat her, and she threatened to leave. A few days after the Sisters' arrival, she made good her threat. Sister Mary assumed the burden of trying to feed girls and staff on eight cents a day per person. Under war-time inflation, this sum would buy a main meal of cheap meat, a vegetable, bread and molasses. Supper would be bread and tea, with a molasses cookie and on occasion a pat of butter. The milk supply depended on one cow, but even when she wandered away at milking time, the Sisters preferred this arrangement to buying milk. Dairies in the sixties were notorious for watering every can of milk, and there was as yet no sanitary code. The Sisters looked back on the simple meals at St. Luke's Hospital as feasts. In the House of Mercy, an early Sister commented wryly, virtue was its own and sole reward.

There were no towels or sheets and none of the girls possessed a change of underclothing. The Sisters set about with their needles to make new clothing and household linens. The clean-up campaign met with some resistance. Early accounts relate vicious fights, swearing and ribald songs as the girls made every effort to defy and shock their new warders. Little by little, though, the dirt disappeared and the Sisters won the respect and affection of the girls. Louisa Cooper, their former associate from St. Luke's, called one day to find Sister Harriet "black as a coal heaver," cleaning out the cellar. She hoped to eliminate the rats, which, to everyone's dismay, sallied forth in platoons every night for bold scampers up and down the stairs. No one but Sister Harriet had courage enough to invade their domain. She was rewarded by the discovery of a heap of scrap iron, which she announced she would sell to get money for furniture. By such efforts, necessities such as cooking pots, chairs and tables were acquired. In later days the Sisters reminisced often and fondly of the old House of Mercy, where even the dog, they said, had only three legs.

The weather that winter was extremely severe, and the little coal they could afford burned far too rapidly in their old and broken stoves. The Sisters wore cloaks inside and prescribed coats and mittens indoors for the girls. In the midst of the bitterest weather, what they called "spotted fever" broke out among the girls, and the Sisters labored night and day nursing them. As the epidemic subsided, Sister Harriet got away long enough to attend the ordination of a friend. To acquaintances who inquired how all was going she replied with characteristic optimism. One of the inquirers was the Rt. Rev. Horatio Potter, Bishop of New York, whom they had approached for permission to organize a Sisterhood. She reminded him that the Sisters were eagerly awaiting his word and hoped to have his official recognition, advice and sanction. He promised to see what could be done and soon after appointed a committee of priests in his diocese to investigate the subject and report to him.

Unfortunately the previous June Sister Jane had asked the Rev. E. Folsom Baker to draw up a rule for a proposed "Sisterhood of St. Catherine" and write a service of admission. By autumn Mr. Baker had finished preparing the reception service and had had it handsomely printed in red and black. Rumor of this service reached Bishop Potter late in October and he wrote Mr. Baker objecting that

> something very formal and somewhat peculiar is proposed to
> be used on occasion of the introduction of a new member into
> the Sisterhood, and that a number of persons have been in-

vited. . . The Sisterhood in its present aspects is entirely new in this Diocese. The whole subject is one of a most delicate nature. The question of a form of initiation has occupied the anxious attention of other Bishops—as indeed the question of having *anything* very formal or public and I should much prefer that the whole matter remain in *statu quo* until I can have time to consider it more carefully.

Mr. Baker hastened to take a copy of the reception service to the Bishop for his approval. The Bishop's permission indicated no intention of his becoming involved in the service:

Having some time since assented informally to the holding of a Service connected with what is called a Sisterhood (without having seen the proposed Service) which Service was to be held in the House of Mercy, I beg now to say that I do not wish to interfere with the holding of that Service, and that I reserve that and all other questions connected with the Sisterhood for future consideration. Under the circumstances perhaps the Chaplain of the House of Mercy will not object to the holding of the Services for this occasion in that Institution—but if he should object, it may be held elsewhere.

New York   Horatio Potter

November 4, 1863

P.S. I feel bound to add, that the Ladies who are devoting themselves to pious and charitable works in the House of Mercy, will have if their measures are wisely and prudently taken, which I will not doubt, my warm approval and sympathy.

H.P.

The chill of this conditional sanction was apparently dispelled by Sister Harriet's warm enthusiasm, for soon after their interview the Bishop named a committee to consider the Sisterhood proposal. The reverend gentlemen named were Isaac Henry Tuttle, Rector of St. Luke's Church in Hudson

Street; Morgan Dix, Rector of Trinity Parish; Arthur Cleveland Coxe, Rector of Calvary Church; A. N. Littlejohn, Rector of Holy Trinity, Brooklyn; and Thomas McClure Peters, Rector of St. Michael's, Bloomingdale. Each member received a list of topics the Bishop wished him to consider:

1. Is it well for the Bishop to recognize a Sisterhood and to stand in some fixed relation to it?
2. If so, what should that relation be?
3. Should there be different classes, such as full Sisters, probationers and associates?
4. With what engagements should a woman enter the Sisterhood?
5. Should the age be beyond a certain limit, and what?
6. As to form and circumstances of initiation—how far a religious solemnity and how far public?
7. As to a uniform habit.
8. How shall the First Sister be appointed, and for what term?
9. Shall there be a Rector between the Sisters and the Bishop?
10. Of what age should he be, and how appointed?
11. Shall the Sisterhood be a general Institution, independent of the House of Mercy, and incorporated?
12. How shall rules, and a form of initiation, be drawn up?
13. Can you suggest a name for the Sisterhood?
14. And as to the function of a Sister, is the term Deaconess a right and expedient one to use?

While the committee considered these matters, Bishop Potter himself wrote the Rt. Rev. William Rollinson Whittingham, Bishop of Maryland, to inquire about the Sisterhood of the Good Shepherd in Baltimore. In reply, Bishop Whittingham alluded to difficulties, personal disagreements and misunderstandings, "of which there have been no few", but

23

commented cheerfully that these neither surprised nor discouraged him. He added:

> I have encountered much of the same difficulty which embarrassed you. . . Although much urged to frame definite rules for permanent obedience, I have not yet believed myself qualified for doing so by adequate experience.

The day chosen for the first meeting of the clerical committee was, as it happened, the Feast of the Purification, destined to be the new Sisterhood's patronal feast. In Morgan Dix's diary for 1864 is this entry:

> February 2nd: At one p.m. the Commission on Sisterhoods met. All present except Mr. Peters (who had to be at the funeral of the Matron of the Bloomingdale asylum, of which he is Chaplain.) We completed our examinations of the Bishop's questions and they appointed me to draw up the report.

Of that report, signed by the committee members and sent off to the Bishop on February 26, nothing is known; Bishop Potter in his address to the Diocesan Convention of 1864 described it merely as "elaborate and instructive." This much is certain: the suggestions Bishop Potter chose to adopt provided a solid foundation upon which a true religious community could rise:

1. That the Bishop recognize the foundation of Sisterhoods, which may be incorporated if necessary.
2. That he be legally visitor of each such foundation with power to impose an Episcopal check on all of their proceedings.
3. That the Bishop draw up a form of reception for the candidates for Sisterhoods.
4. That he appoint a Chaplain for the Sisters.

5. That the Sisters wear a suitable uniform habit.
6. That the Sisters choose a name for their organization, and draw up a code of rules, subject to the Bishop's approval.
7. That the work of a Sister be not limited, but be held to include all the corporal and spiritual works of mercy which a woman may perform, and that the idea as well of a contemplative life of prayer and devotion as of an active life of labor be included in the office, but especially that the Sisters be devoted to the care of the sick and needy and to the work of educating the young.

On June 26, 1864, the Bishop visited the House of Mercy for confirmation, taking tea with the Sisters afterward. Favorably impressed, he appointed Dr. Tuttle of St. Luke's Church to be Chaplain of the House, and at the Diocesan Convention in the autumn he made an impassioned appeal for funds for the Sisters.

Encouraged, the Sisters on October 6, 1864, assumed the management of an orphanage at Ninety-ninth Street, the Sheltering Arms. Its organizer was the gifted rector of St. Michael's, Bloomingdale, the Rev. Thomas McClure Peters. He persuaded Sister Harriet to abandon tentative plans for a children's hospital in order that she and Sister Amelia Asten, who had joined them, might take over a shelter for children from infancy to twelve years. Women prisoners to whom he ministered had pleaded with Mr. Peters to care for their children, whom they were forced to surrender either to public charity, which they dreaded, or to Roman Catholic institutions, which then required relinquishing of custody. Another kind of need was represented by the case of a blind toddler named Minnie, found abandoned on the steps of City Hall; she could not be placed in a blind asylum because she was too young and was refused admission by all the orphanages because she was blind. Mr. Peters had prevailed upon the Sisters to care for Minnie at the House of Mercy until an institution could be opened for her and the other destitute cases which confronted him.

Mr. Peters first announced to his family that they were moving from their spacious Greek-revival mansion at Ninety-ninth Street, Bloomingdale. He then granted a fifteen-year lease free of rent to the Sheltering Arms of Jesus, a name suggested by his friend, Dr. Muhlenberg. With his usual dispatch, Mr. Peters persuaded the Sisters to take over, enlisted the aid of twenty-one New York business men as trustees, and asked Miss Ellen Kemble to form a Ladies' Association to meet monthly and provide support.

With two Sisters at the Sheltering Arms, the year 1864 ended with the Community-to-be established in two works. On Sunday, December 10, Dr. Dix called at the House of Mercy to administer the sacraments to a dying girl and to celebrate the Holy Communion for the other thirty-one inmates, two Sisters, some probationers and one or two guests. Sister Jane welcomed him warmly, and he wrote in his diary that the service "was one of the most interesting I have ever seen or had a part in." It was after two o'clock before he arrived at his parents' home on Twenty-first Street, very late for dinner. Obviously, he was no longer cooly detached about the Sisterhood venture as he had been the previous June when Sister Jane had written Mr. Baker, "I feel as if (Dr. Dix) rather thought us a bother, with little confidence in us."

His diary entry for February 1, 1865, noted that Dr. Tuttle had sent him the form to be used the next day for the reception of Jane Haight, Mary Heartt, Amelia Asten, Sarah

26

Bridge and Harriet Cannon into the Sisterhood of Saint Mary, the name chosen by Bishop Potter. Dr. Dix read the form with sincere thankfulness "for the steady progress which we are making."

St. Michael's Church, Bloomingdale, where the first profession took place on February 2, 1865, was a churchly Victorian structure of tongue-and-groove

Plans to hold a great benefit-bazaar to help finance this new building in Manhattanville for the Sheltering Arms involved the Sisters in a controversy which forced their resignation in 1870. Vague charges of "ritualism" were hurled.

siding, and was surrounded by a spacious burial ground. A towering stone church now stands on the same site, at Amsterdam and Ninety-ninth Street.

Mother Harriet in two variations of the habit worn by early Sisters of Saint Mary. Modifications made about 1870 covered the Sisters' hair and provided a veil for outdoor wear, over an English "cottage straw bonnet".

CHAPTER THREE

Genesis

T HE DAY IN NEW YORK was clear and cold, and Horace Greeley's *Tribune* predicted that the ground-hog would see his shadow. The newspapers that Thursday morning, February 2, 1865, cited rumors that Confederate peace negotiators had passed through Union lines under a flag of truce. Maryland was announced as the first state to ratify the amendment abolishing slavery, and crushed sugar had soared to thirty-one cents a pound. Booth was starring in *Hamlet* at the Winter Garden, and Barnum's American Museum lured customers with a mammoth monkey, a fat woman and two glass steam engines in motion.

In mid-morning Morgan Dix strode cross-town to Eighth Avenue and waited in a stiff north wind for the horse car. Tall and dignified at thirty-eight, Dr. Dix was more than usually absorbed in thought today. If one war was ending, he knew, another was about to begin. The Bishop's sponsorship of the Sisterhood would no doubt draw fire, and Morgan Dix was prepared to give him every support.

From Fifty-ninth Street, where the horse cars turned back, he had a two-mile walk to St. Michael's Church, Bloomingdale, a quaint little gothic building of vertical tongue-and-groove siding. He walked through the churchyard with its scattered gravestones and picket fence and into the sacristy, where he joined the reverend clerics: Littlejohn, Tuttle, Howland, Stansbury, Neide, Williams and Peters. Bishop Potter greeted him warmly, his face pale above his high old-fashioned clerical stock.

The Sisters from the House of Mercy were relieved when Sister Harriet appeared, for she had been isolated with a small boy critically ill with smallpox. Still quarantined on February 2, she ordered fresh clothing, left careful instructions to an attendant, and hurried across to St. Michael's Church.

The service at noon had been arranged by the Bishop himself; it was he who had chosen St. Mary as their patroness and the Feast of the Purification as the day of their profession. After the Creed, a hymn was sung while the five candidates rose and stood before the Bishop. He addressed them briefly and questioned them regarding their willingness to live in obedience and persevere in the work of the Lord. When these questions had been satisfactorily answered, the candidates knelt. The Bishop and priests formed a circle around them and recited antiphonally the hymn *Veni Creator Spiritus*. Following collects and other prayers, the Bishop took each Sister by the right hand and received her for the work of God into the fellowship of the Sisterhood of Saint Mary. The Bishop then gave each Sister his episcopal blessing and resumed the celebration of the Eucharist. After the service, the Sisters and their friends gathered for lunch at the House of

Mercy. At five o'clock, Sister Harriet was back at her nursing post.

It is doubtful that the participants in the reception service were fully aware of its significance. Not since the dissolution of the English monasteries in the sixteenth century had an Anglican Bishop dared to stand in a parish church and officially constitute a religious community, and one, more-over, designed to be a true monastic body, not a philanthropic sorority. Once he had decided to sponsor the Sisterhood of Saint Mary, Bishop Potter never looked back. His close ad-visers warned that attack would follow. He replied that the worst criticism could be forestalled by omitting public, formal vows. The Sisters therefore made promises which, though regarded as of lifelong obligation, were called *revocable.* This enabled the Bishop to reassure the excited at the Diocesan Convention the following autumn:

> I need scarcely say that in the Association there are no irre-vocable vows, no engagements which could interfere to prevent their return to ordinary positions in life, should any claim of duty from friends or relatives unexpectedly arise to require it. In the meantime, they have a recognized and protected posi-tion, they have the strength and consolation that comes from feeling that they are wholly dedicated to a holy work, and they are so sequestered from trivial cares and interruptions that they can give themselves with tenfold efficiency to their labors of love.

The Community by-laws expressly stated that no Sister should be required to take irrevocable vows. This left the way clear for Sisters to take the three-fold vows privately, if they wished. From the first profession until March 25, 1873, each Sister made her life vows individually and privately to her confessor some months, or even some years, after her public profession. The six Sisters professed on Lady Day, 1873, made their life vows publicly the following August 29 in St. Michael's Chapel of the old St. Mary's Convent, Peekskill; Father C. C. Grafton, S.S.J.E., received their vows and gave them the cross and ring. This prepared the way for the vows to be incorporated into the Profession Office. The by-laws provision still held, however, and Sister Thecla, professed on July 2, 1873, elected not to take the three-fold vows, finding in the Profession Office a sufficient expression of her dedication. She alone among the Sisters wore no knots in her girdle, but her profession was sealed by death in 1878 when she died nursing the victims of yellow fever in Memphis.

II

Such sagacity as Bishop Potter displayed regarding the vows enabled him to advise, steady and chasten the infant Community and bring it safely through the furor ahead. It is strange and sad that the Sisters who owe him so great a debt should know so little about him. He shrank from public notice, left no literary monument and has, regrettably, no biography. He is scarcely mentioned in the biographies of his older brother Alonzo, Bishop of Pennsylvania, and of his nephew, Henry Codman Potter, his successor in the See of New York. Yet the impressive dimensions of Horatio Potter emerge in every event in which he played a decisive role.

He was born in 1802, the youngest child of nine born to Joseph and Anne Potter, Quaker farmers living near Beekman in Dutchess County, New York. Their Quaker devotion appears in the names they bestowed on their oldest son,

Paraclete, and only daughter, Philadelphia. Their son Alonzo was the first to become an Episcopalian. Following his graduation from Union College, Schenectady, he worked in Philadelphia at a book-shop owned by his brother Sheldon, and while there was baptized in St. Peter's Church by Bishop William White and began to study for the ministry. In 1819, aged nineteen, Alonzo returned to Union College to teach mathematics and natural philosophy. At this time Horatio, tired of his mercantile career, appealed to Alonzo for help in obtaining a college education. With that help, Horatio graduated from Union College in 1826, was confirmed by Bishop Hobart at St. Thomas' Church in New York and began studying for holy orders. In 1828 Horatio was ordained priest and became professor of mathematics and natural philosophy at Washington College, now Trinity College, Hartford, Connecticut.

In 1833, Horatio Potter began his twenty-one-year rectorship of St. Peter's Church, Albany, years in which he effected

> the passage from the old to the modern methods of Church thought and work, and educated the parish in the principles of Catholic theology and sound Churchmanship.

The transition included removal of the three-decker pulpit from its central position in the sanctuary, and the introduction of gas lamps to replace the candles which slaves had placed in sconces beside the pews of the wealthy.

The years in Albany were marked by sickness and sorrow. In 1830, the Potters' oldest child, a two-year-old son, died. In 1834, their four-year-old daughter Mary died. In 1835, worn out by sickness and parochial burdens, he sailed for England, carrying letters of introduction to Bishop Skinner of the

33

Scottish Episcopal Church, and other notables including John Keble. He returned much refreshed, and in 1837 declined the presidency of Washington College to continue parish work. His sermons were noted for "vigor of thought, purity of style and elegance of diction," the parish historian wrote, and this in a period of what Dr. Potter called "barndoor eloquence." Called to address the New York State Assembly at the death of President Harrison in 1841, he delivered, instead of a conventional eulogy, a probing analysis of the evils of political life.

In 1845 the Potters both visited England, where they stayed with John Keble and with Isaac Williams, poet of the Catholic Revival. Both, Dr. Potter wrote home, "were men of singular modesty, purity and devotion." He noted rumors that Newman was expected to submit to Roman Catholicism, adding that Dr. Pusey was "standing fast." The Potters were invited to visit Dr. Pusey at Christ Church, Oxford, enroute to Liverpool, and on September 15 Dr. Potter wrote:

> Yesterday we had the Communion with him in the Cathedral. ——————, and I, and —————— pray with him in his study five or six times a day. Such meekness and love, such a contrite and broken spirit, it has not before been my fortune to meet.

Alluding to the 1845 trial of the Rt. Rev. B. T. Onderdonk, Bishop of New York, on immorality charges brought by his ecclesiastical enemies, Dr. Potter wrote "Each party, I think, would soon ruin itself, but for the violence and blunders of the opposite."

With Bishop Onderdonk sentenced to suspension from the exercise of his ministry and of his office as bishop, a heavy weight fell on Dr. Potter in the oversight of the missions in upstate New York, and this at a time of personal grief. In 1847 Mary Jane Tomlinson Potter, his gentle and quiet wife, died, leaving six children, five of them under twelve. Dr. Potter saw in his loss the loving purposes of God:

> It is my earnest prayer to Him who makes use of suffering as a means of instruction and sanctification that he would be pleased by the teaching of this heavy trial to impart more depth and spiritual wisdom as well as more earnestness and tenderness to all my efforts to edify and console the beloved people of my spiritual charge.

In 1852 the Diocese finally elected Jonathan Wainwright as Provisional Bishop, thereby enabling Dr. Potter to take a holiday in Scotland. During this trip he met Mary Atchison Pollock, a retiring Scottish lady of forty-two with whom he continued to correspond after his return to Albany. In 1853 she accepted his proposal of marriage and arrived in New York, where Dr. Potter met her at the dock and escorted her to Trinity Church for their wedding.

In 1854, Bishop Wainwright died, worn out by the arduous labors of repairing the neglect caused by the seven years' vacancy in the episcopate. At the Diocesan Convention that followed, Dr. Potter was elected Bishop on the ninth ballot. In his acceptance speech, he pleaded with his fellow Churchmen to "try to love each other, try to banish hard words, and satirical speeches, and uncharitable judgments from the Church of God. . ."

In his long episcopate he demonstrated heroic strength and restraint. His nephew and successor, also a great ecclesiastical statesman, cited

> a singular wisdom and meekness in his episcopate and his

habitual reserve was one of its largest elements of strength, founded upon a sounder conception of the Church as a church, and not as a sect, than was understood by those who misjudged his patience and forbearance.

It was such a man who stepped forward to sponsor the Community, in a time of spiritual decline and public corruption. It would be pleasant to think that among the Sisters he found understanding and appreciation of the difficulty of his position, but they too mistook his caution for timidity. Only in retrospect did Mother Harriet see it clearly. Had she never known Bishop Potter, she told a younger Sister, she would have missed her religious vocation.

HOUSES OF C.S.M.

INDICATING: CONVENTS ▬, Houses —, & Subordinate Houses —

1860 1870 1880 1890 1900 1910 1920 1930 1940 1950 1960

House of Mercy—St. Mary's-in-the-Field*
    At 86th St., Manhattan
    At Inwood, Manhattan
    At Valhalla, N.Y.
Sheltering Arms
St. Barnabas House
St. Mary's School, Manhattan
St. Mary's School, Mt. St. Gabriel, Peekskill
St. Gabriel's School, Peekskill
The Junior School, Peekskill
St. Mary's Hospital
    At 34th St., Manhattan
    At Bayside, N.Y.
   Noyes Memorial Home, Peekskill
   St. Mary's-by-the-Sea, Far Rockaway, N.Y.
   St. Mary's Summer Hospital, Norwalk, Conn.
Laura Franklin Hospital, Manhattan
ST. MARY'S CONVENT, PEEKSKILL
   Marycroft
Church Orphans' Home, Memphis
   Church Orphans' Summer Home, Fayetteville, Ark.
St. Mary's School, Memphis
IN TRINITY PARISH
    Trinity Infirmary, Manhattan
    Trinity Mission House, Manhattan
    Trinity Seaside Home, Great River, N.Y.
Kemper Hall, Kenosha, Wis.
ST. MARY'S CONVENT, KENOSHA, WIS.
St. Mary's Mission, Chicago
St. Mary's Home, Chicago†
   St. Mary's Summer Home, Kenosha‡
St. Mary's-on-the-Mountain, Sewanee, Tenn.
ST. MARY'S CONVENT, SEWANEE
House of Mercy, Washington, D.C.
St. Katharine's School, Davenport, Iowa
St. Mary's Mission, Sagada, Philippine Islands
St. Luke's Mission, Rutherfordton, N.C.
St. Raphael's House, Evergreen, Colo.
De Koven Foundation, Racine, Wis.
House of the Redeemer, Manhattan
Ascension Parish School, Sierra Madre, Calif.

1860 1870 1880 1890 1900 1910 1920 1930 1940 1950 1960

*Name changed in 1938
‡At Libertyville, Ill., 1925-1930; at Racine, Wis., 1933-
†At Elmhurst, Ill., 1922-1923.

------Summer only

Points which figured in the early years are shown on the map of Manhattan (right). Strictly localized at first, the Sister's apostolate eventually included seven dioceses, with temporary houses in other dioceses as well. Over the century, Sisters of Saint Mary lived and worked in some thirty-eight houses, indicated on chart (above). (Map and chart by Joan White.)

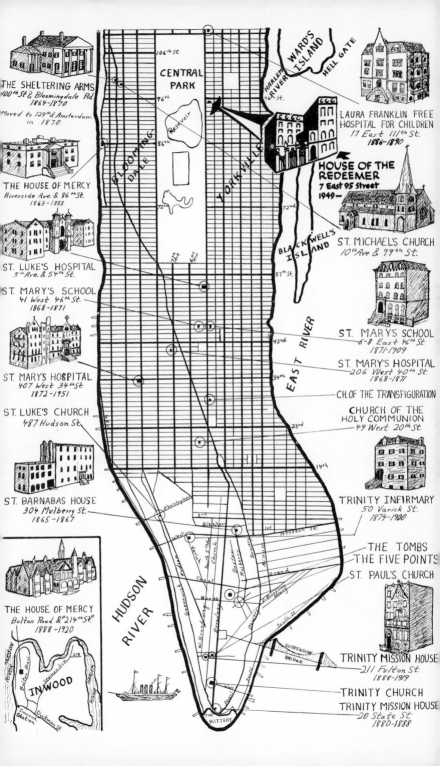

THE SHELTERING ARMS
100th St. & Bloomingdale Rd.
1864-1870

Moved to 129th & Amsterdam
in 1870

THE HOUSE OF MERCY
Riverside Ave. & 86th St.
1863-1888

ST. LUKE'S HOSPITAL
5th Ave. & 54th St.

ST. MARY'S SCHOOL
41 West 46th St.
1868-1871

ST. MARY'S HOSPITAL
407 West 34th St.
1872-1951

ST. LUKE'S CHURCH
487 Hudson St.

ST. BARNABAS HOUSE
304 Mulberry St.
1865-1867

THE HOUSE OF MERCY
Bolton Road & "214th St."
1888-1920

INWOOD

HUDSON RIVER

CENTRAL PARK

106th St.

96th

Reservoir

86th

72nd

BLOOMINGDALE

YORKVILLE

WARD'S ISLAND

HARLEM RIVER

HELL GATE

LAURA FRANKLIN FREE
HOSPITAL FOR CHILDREN
17 East 111th St.
1886-1890

HOUSE OF THE
REDEEMER
7 East 95 Street
1949 —

ST. MICHAEL'S CHURCH
10th Ave. & 99th St.

BLACKWELL'S ISLAND

EAST RIVER

ST. MARY'S SCHOOL
6-8 East 46th St.
1871-1909

ST. MARY'S HOSPITAL
206 West 40th St.
1868-1871

CH. OF THE TRANSFIGURATION

CHURCH OF THE
HOLY COMMUNION
49 West 20th St.

TRINITY INFIRMARY
50 Varick St.
1874-1900

THE TOMBS
THE FIVE POINTS

ST. PAUL'S CHURCH

TRINITY MISSION HOUSE
211 Fulton St.
1888-1919

TRINITY CHURCH

TRINITY MISSION HOUSE
20 State St.
1880-1888

THE BATTERY

SUSPENSION BRIDGE

57th St.

42nd

34th

23rd

14th

CHAPTER FOUR

Beginning

THE YEARS IMMEDIATELY FOLLOWING the first Profession were marked by events indicating the direction of the Community's development, events the more absorbing because they were happening for the first time, impressing the five Sisters again and again with the blessedness of their new life.

On June 11, 1865, the Feast of Saint Barnabas, Miss Elizabeth Greene received the habit as Sister Agnes, becoming the Community's first Novice.

That same day the Sisters undertook a third work, St. Barnabas' House at 304 Mulberry Street on Manhattan's Lower East Side. Mrs. Richmond had founded the House for homeless women and children, probably intending it as a reception center for the House of Mercy. With her characteristic zeal, Mrs. Richmond rented a building in the heart of the vice district, close to Police Headquarters, and searched the streets at night for women in need of haven. Her illness forced her to turn the work over to the City Mission Society, which in turn called the Sisters. Sister Mary was placed in charge.

Organization of the Midnight Mission as a rescue work in the vice district enabled Sister Mary to concentrate on providing shelter for women whose only crime was homelessness. In 1866 some fifty-one thousand meals and lodgings were provided on a budget of $3,889, and the adjoining building at 306 Mulberry was purchased for a childrens' dormitory, a day nursery and chapel. The City Mission Report praised the Sisters

> whose care of the inmates and prudent management of its affairs neither price could reward nor praise equal.

Destitution was the only qualification for admission. The House was included in a long feature, "Afternoon Visits to Asylums for Fallen Virtue" in the *New York Citizen* late in 1866. Of the five shelters visited, two were operated by Protestants and two by the Sisters of Saint Mary; but one, the Convent of the Good Shepherd, a Roman Catholic institution, enrolled two hundred of the three hundred women cared for by all five institutions, a fact noted with some asperity.

Though the reporter praised St. Barnabas' House as "a most benevolent and worthy undertaking," she reserved her highest tribute for the House of Mercy, in an account which affords a unique view of the earliest Sisters, attired in

> black dress, white linen collars, with square frontal ends, Quakeristical tissue-like caps, with tissue pendants, placed over plainly-parted hair.

The author praised the tasteful arrangements of the rooms, with flowers, books and pictures, adding

40

there is an aristocratic hue which seems to gild the entire house. The Lady Superior gave me a welcome and showed me very courteously to all parts of that most beautiful, homelike Retreat. . . I passed up a back staircase to find three dormitories with twelve beds in each, all neatly arranged with mattresses, snowy coverlids and pillow-cases. The sewing-room, the wash-room, with its half dozen marble basins and the accoutrements, the laundry-room and its shelves of nicely arranged clothes; the school-room, with its desks and appurtenances; the infirmary and the store-closets, all in excellent order, were thrown open for my inspection. . . The Lady Superior, benign and bland, imparting instructions or giving commands, was received respectfully and kindly. Orderliness, neatness and decency were observed. The inmates suitably clothed and plainly dressed. This asylum must be visited to be appreciated; it surely will call forth the encomiums of all churchmen—a sufficient test of what religious influences, gratuitously given, can accomplish.

II

In September, 1865, the Sisters convened their first Chapter in the sacristy of St. Luke's, Hudson Street, and elected Sister Harriet as Superior. That they waited nearly eight months before taking this step reflected painful memories of the Sisterhood of the Holy Communion; it also indicated the hope that Sister Jane's health might improve sufficiently to enable her to accept the position. To Mr. Baker, Sister Jane pointed out that the Superior's job was an unenviable one for which she doubted her qualification, but the brisk, managerial tone of her letters indicates that the Sisters deferred to her judgment on Community questions. As early as 1863 she wrote:

We do indeed want to have all things on a right foundation this time. . . We want it to have the interest and confidence of the Church—and have the Bishop for our Spiritual Head. . . About going to England—I do not quite see how we could do that. I think Miss Ayres visited all Houses in England and on the Continent. You see what hers came to. Besides I think Miss Sellon's (early English Sisterhood) was a failure—she assuming too much power. I believe the Clergy decline to have anything to do with it. Miss Ayres is my authority—and I have also seen a book called "The experience of a Sister of Mercy." Our rules should be few, simple and as free from unnatural restraint as possible. Love the ruling and underlying principle. I think the great mistake has been too great strictness in things of no moment, making a life of good works, freely given to God, a life of unnatural restraint and almost bondage.

Though ill from the tuberculosis which caused her death in 1868, Sister Jane acted always with immense energy and enthusiasm. She called in the Rev. John Henry Hopkins, Jr., deacon and brilliant artist-journalist son of the Bishop of Vermont, to advise them on redecorating the House of Mercy chapel. She dispatched the attorney of a "scamp plumber" who had tried to fleece them. A youthful house-painter who left a note to two of the girls in the House asking them to meet him on the River bank she outwitted by sending two police officers to meet him, instead. She persuaded Dr. Milo Mahan, distinguished professor at the General Theological Seminary, to come and preach to the girls, reporting to Mr. Baker afterward that if she could find such a chaplain as Dr. Mahan, the girls would respond readily to Christian teaching.

Able as she was, it was sadly evident by September that Sister Jane was too ill for additional responsibilities. The Sisters gathered in her sick-room from time to time to discuss with utmost informality the question of organization. There was general agreement that Sister Harriet should be their presiding officer, but by what title to call her? They were determined it should not be "First Sister," and settled finally on "Superior."

The formal Chapter, in the presence of their Chaplain, Dr. Tuttle, probably lasted no longer than ten minutes. Had some forecast indicated that the sacristy where they gathered would one day be a Blessed Sacrament chapel with an exquisite statue of Sister Harriet, the Sisters doubtless would have dismissed the idea as utter fantasy. From the brief business meeting they hurried back to their several responsibilities; Sister Harriet assumed her new role by setting about to acquire some knowledge of the religious life.

It was a characteristic beginning, for until her death she was always reaching out, listening, learning. This pliancy, openness and readiness to move ahead was to benefit her Community in the three decades she served as its Superior. Another notable characteristic was her patient forbearance, a quality seldom displayed by Sister Jane.

Accordingly, Sisters Harriet and Sarah traveled to Baltimore to visit the Sisterhood of the Good Shepherd. Sister Catherine, the Superior, received them courteously but was unable to offer much help. They did, however, bring away some satisfactory instructions for postulants, drawn up by the Rev. C. W. Rankin, Chaplain of the Baltimore Sisterhood. These were put to immediate use, for Catharine Hassett was received as a postulant on July 3, 1866, the same day that Miss Edna Baker, sister of the Rev. E. Folsom Baker, received the habit.

One of Sister Jane's letters to Mr. Baker affords an illuminating glimpse of the free relations between Superior and Sisters at this time:

> Mrs. Tyler is staying in town. You know she is the Superior of the Baltimore Sisterhood. I suspect she would like to join us or work with us. Sister Harriet proposed her coming to help me but I declined; then she desired Sister Mary to allow her to work at St. Barnabas, but Sister M. had the same opinion that I had—she was pleasant as a visitor and *that* she had best remain.

III

On their first anniversary, February 2, 1866, Dr. Tuttle resigned as Chaplain, pleading his parochial duties. Dr. Thomas M. Peters was proposed to the Bishop as Dr. Tuttle's successor, but a timely interview with Sister Harriet brought about the appointment of Dr. Dix instead.

Morgan Dix was eminently well qualified to foster the Community through its infancy. So devoted was he to the project of reviving the religious life that he never shrank even when the Sisters themselves failed him. His great faith, his astute mind and splendid scholarship, his devotion to principle and his serene conviction, even his social eminence, assured position and family name, made him invulnerable to attack from enemies who would have scrupled at nothing to destroy him.

His grandfather, Colonel Timothy Dix of Boscawen, New Hampshire, was a Puritan with extraordinarily broad views; he sent his son John Adams Dix to a Roman Catholic College in Montreal to learn French and to encounter another culture. The boy grew up to marry an Episcopalian, the daughter of a wealthy landowner in Cooperstown, N.Y., and to attain eminence as statesman and military commander. He served as Secretary of State in Albany from 1833 to 1839 and as United States Senator from 1845 to 1850. His pronounced anti-slavery views kept him from higher office in the Democratic administrations preceding the Civil War. Even so, he was called to take over the Treasury Department in the final, frantic days of the Buchanan administration and restored order out of the chaos left by his secessionist predecessor. As a Major General and Commander of the Department of the East, John Adams Dix restored law enforcement and order following the draft riots in New York in 1863. His integrity was never questioned, and his distinction as a public servant went far toward protecting his son from assault.

The son was equally vigorous and forceful. Before his ordination he kept an all-night vigil. His mother confided to a friend that Morgan had foresworn as unsuitable to his calling the theatre, smoking, owning a carriage and hunting ducks on the salt flats of Long Island.

His relationship with Bishop Potter was one of mutual confidence and affection, springing from the Albany years when the Dix family had attended St. Peter's Church.

Moreover, Morgan Dix shared the Sisters' interest in Catholic renewal. He noted with distaste the priests who officiated in black gown and salt-and-pepper gloves, a common clerical costume. He exulted in the splendour of Trinity Church's Ascension festival, with symphony orchestra and choir rendering Gounod's *Messe Solennelle.* Nor was his interest merely aesthetic. He wrote:

It may be demonstrated by historical evidence that distaste for

45

the solemn splendours and calm loveliness of Catholic worship leads inevitably to rejection of the dogmas of our Creed and the revolt from that divine law which regulates the moral actions of men.

On April 4, 1866, Dr. Dix presented the Sisters with their first Rule, which with their amendments and alterations, was sent to the Bishop for his approval. On the Second Sunday after Epiphany, the Sisters recited Vespers from their new breviary, the *Book of Hours,* which Dr. Dix had begun compiling a year earlier. Prior to this time they used a small book containing Prime and Compline, the first and final Offices of the day. Now, to their delight, they could recite the day hours of the breviary.

The storm was not long in breaking. In the unsigned preface to the *Book of Hours,* Dr. Dix had explained that the compilation had been made for the use of

> persons . . . called of the Holy Ghost to give themselves up to charitable and religious works, as the Apostle expressed it, to continue in supplications and prayers night and day.

This mild allusion inspired the *Recorder* to demand:

> Have we then a community of monks of our communion? If we have, where is it? Do any of our Bishops know of its existence, and sanction it? It would be a singular thing to find an institution which all the enlightened catholics in Europe regard as the most stupid and corrupting nuisance in the church, and which they are laboring, not without success, to abate, springing up in the midst of a Protestant church in a republican government.

The *Church Times* broke the news that the "Father Ignatius" of the new community was none other than the "rector of the most powerful ecclesiastical corporation in the United States", and warned:

We now learn where old Trinity stands, and what we are to expect of her in the future; and also what is to be the policy of the Romanizers. It now remains to be seen whether such things are to be passed over by the Bishop of the Diocese unrebuked.

One editor quoted the hymn "Virgin-born, we bow before Thee," as evidence of the "mawkish mariolatry" in the *Book of Hours,* eliciting from the *Church Journal* the cool comment

> . . . as the Hymn in question was written by Bishop Heber, all that can be inferred from it is that Dr. Dix is as terrible a Romanizer as Bishop Heber!

Thus the polemicists were ready when the Profession of Sister Agnes was received by Bishop Potter on May 22 in St. Luke's Church. The *World* and other secular papers called the service a "consecration", which inspired the editor of *The Episcopalian* to point out that there had been no imposition of hands:

> Hands were raised, and waved; hands were shaken and squeezed; hands were folded, pointed, and crossed, but they were not *imposed*. There was no episcopal, apostolic contact, and hence no grace was communicated and imparted.

Nor was Sister Agnes ordained, the editor insisted, because "tonsure, chrism and contact of holy hands were wanting." More telling than either of these quite admissible allegations was the editor's deft exposure of the nature of the promises:

> The *vows* were not quite up to the conventional (sic) and historic precedents. . . Miss Agnes is committed to nothing. She had no indelible character impressed. She is not ordained, is not consecrated; she is only an 'almost' nun, and almost the bride of the Bishop. . . She may look as forlorn and uncouth as

47

the veritable sisters, but she is not one, and we hope she never will be. . .

A lesser man than Morgan Dix might have faltered before the attacks which these reports provoked, but he showed no sign of halting. He defended the Sisters in a long letter to the *Church Journal,* signed "D", as "the first Diocesan Sisterhood in the American Church, paltering with no Protestant names, and playing with no Roman extravagance." That summer of 1866 Sister Sarah made her first confession to Dr. Dix, and the others followed. The oratories at the Sheltering Arms and St. Barnabas' House were blessed in services prepared and conducted by Dr. Dix. Rumors that the militant protestants were ready to challenge the Sisterhood at the Diocesan Convention in the autumn failed to move him, though the *World* reported:

> The ministers opposed to the sisterhood have held several meetings in their rooms at the Bible House, and they have resolved to present the whole subject before the Diocesan Convention. . . . Happily for the good Sisters of St. Mary, the convention has no power to cite them to appear in St. John's Chapel during their sessions, and answer such questions as might be propounded to them, relative to the alleged vows of celibacy they have taken.

Whatever attack was planned did not appear at the Convention; but the plotters had other weapons, and soon used them.

The old Convent at Peekskill in the seventies, connecting with St. Gabriel's School.

The first Trinity Mission House near the tip of Manhattan at Battery Park.

St. Mary's Free Hospital for Children, showing first addition to the building.

Harper's Young People, March 26, 1889, carried this engraving of a cot endowed by its young readers' contributions. The sign on the wall carries the date 1883, with the inscription, "Little children, love one another."

CHAPTER FIVE

Advance

A S THE NEW YEAR 1867 BEGAN, Sister Harriet was critically ill with typhoid fever. In thanksgiving for her recovery, she made formal life vows on February 2, 1867, in St. Paul's Chapel, an hour before the service commemorating the Community's second anniversary. She knelt before the splendid white and gold "Glory" of L'Enfant's altarpiece, with clouds and lighting enclosing the tablets of the Law, surmounted by the Hebrew word for God. There, in the presence of Dr. Dix, Sister Harriet repeated the solemn promises he had written, the same words repeated by every Sister of Saint Mary at her Profession:

> In the Name of God, Amen. I, Sister——————, desiring to consecrate myself more fully and entirely than I have hitherto done in body, soul, and spirit, unto the service of our Blessed Lord and Savior, Jesus Christ, do hereby make unto Almighty God, before the company of heaven, and in the presence of you, my spiritual father, the three-fold vow of Celibacy, of

51

Poverty and of Obedience, steadfastly purposing to keep and observe the same unto my life's end, the Lord being my helper; and herein I humbly pray for the grace and heavenly assistance of the Holy Ghost, through Jesus Christ our Lord. Amen.

After the anniversary service, the Sisters and some forty guests enjoyed a lunch provided from the Astor House. "Everything," Dr. Dix wrote in his diary, with evident relief, "passed off pleasantly."

His uneasiness stemmed from criticism directed by the City Mission Board at the undefined horror of "ritualism" at St. Barnabas' House. An investigation was launched. The Sisters had agreed at the outset to assume management for two years; as the expiration of the term approached, Sister Harriet appealed to Dr. Dix to help frame a suitable letter declining to renew the arrangement. He supplied a tactful paragraph to be inserted in Sister Harriet's note offering to withdraw on June 11. This offer was accepted, doubtless with relief, and the Sisters departed from the House, leaving it in the management of Miss Ellen Hulme. In 1869, Miss Hulme organized an evangelical sisterhood, the Sisterhood of the Good Shepherd, which attracted wide approval for the simplicity of its customs and chapel appointments. Public devotions were limited to noon-day prayers in a chapel neatly carpeted, with chairs and a reading desk, but containing no images, pictures or ornaments of any kind.

Sister Harriet was abroad at the time of the departure from St. Barnabas' House on June 11. She had sailed for England on May 18, accompanied by the novice Sister Edna, who thought a trip abroad might help settle her doubts concerning her vocation. They apparently carried gold coin to cover expenses, for Dr. Dix wrote of taking five hundred dollars in gold up to St. Barnabas' House, where it was offered at the Eucharist for the trip. It was an excellent investment. Free of work for the first time in several years, the Superior rested and recovered her health. She visited many English convents, including the Community of St. John Baptist in Clewer, the Sisters of St. Margaret in East Grinstead, the Community of St. Mary at the Cross in Shoreditch, the All Saints' Sisters of the Poor in London and Ascot Priory. She carried letters of introduction from Bishop Potter and Dr. Dix. Among those whom she consulted were Canon T. T. Carter of Clewer and Father Charles C. Grafton, the Bostonian who was one of the three original members of the Society of St. John the Evangelist. Father Grafton urged Sister Harriet to enter the novitiate of an English community, but after serious consideration, she rejected this proposal.

She returned alone to New York on September 18. Sister Edna had entered the novitiate of the Community of St. John the Baptist; after her profession, she came to America as a member of the affiliated American house. Sister Harriet brought her Sisters copies of the Clewer Manual, private devotions for nuns prepared by Canon Carter; and she entertained them at length with tales of her travels.

She had learned much in four months. The first innovation she proposed was a four-day retreat, held in October with Father Grafton as conductor. At its conclusion the conductor received them into the Confraternity of the Blessed Sacrament, an English devotional society not yet established in the United States. A century later the Community retained this connection, so that every Sister is automatically a member of the Confraternity.

Other ideas bore fruit in the months that followed. On the

Feast of All Saints the first "Grey Sisters" were admitted, Sisters Maria Roberts and Catharine Anderson. They were to assist the Sisters by prayer and alms, and were expected to spend one month a year in residence in one of the Houses of the Community.

Also, the habit was apparently modified, for a descriptive pamphlet of 1868 specified a plainly made black serge gown with a plain, deep overcape of the same color and material reaching down about four inches below the waist; and on the street, a long black cloak, and a black English Cottage straw bonnet with black veil.

When Sister Harriet described the convent schools she had seen, the Sisters agreed it would be a good plan to acquire a school, where the Community might have a home of its own. Soon after their decision, early in 1868, Dr. J. J. Elmendorf, founder of a girls' school, Hobart Hall, received an appointment to a post at Racine College, Racine, Wisconsin. He approached the Sisters about taking over his school. This entailed little more than the transfer of eighteen pupils, for the school had lost its lease and its equipment. Such a situation as this always called forth from Sister Harriet the daring lurking beneath her quiet conservatism. "One could never be sure," her biographer wrote, "where her love of adventure with its risks came to an end and where her great faith in God began."

Accompanied by Sister Agnes, Sister Harriet combed Manhattan for a suitable building, finally selecting a house at 41 West Forty-sixth Street. The annual rent was $3,500, and they were penniless. Undaunted, they engaged it and made plans to begin classes. Miss Ellen Kemble collected money for furniture and rent, enabling them to open St. Mary's School on May 1, 1868. Sister Agnes was Mistress of Studies, assisted by Sister Catharine. On the Feast of St. Barnabas, June 11, just one year after their departure from St. Barnabas' House, the oratory of St. Mary's School was blessed; for the first time they had an altar to call their own. Dr. Dix officiated, assisted by Dr. George Seymour and the Rev. Thomas McKee Brown. Absent from the happy gathering were Sister Jane, now critically ill, and Sister Mary, her nurse.

On July 25, Sister Jane died. Her courage, her flashing wit, her intense creativity, made her death most keenly felt. It was she who had planned their parties and resolved their differences; when the doctor prescribed bourbon several times a day, and no talking, she had complained that bourbon loosened "the unruly member." Now she was gone, and it was the Sisters' sad duty to accompany her body up the Hudson to the Haight family plot at Catskill, with Dr. Seymour to officiate.

It was on this trip, with the Sisters making a quiet little group amid the gaiety of the excursion-boat passengers, that Dr. Seymour recognized a priest of his acquaintance and approached to speak. The priest turned abruptly and walked away. Later Dr. Seymour received from the man an apology for his behavior, explaining that it wouldn't do for him to be seen speaking with a man who was accompanied by the Sisters of Saint Mary.

II

Dr. Seymour was not deterred from his devotion to the House of Mercy by snubs. Three times a week he traveled the four miles from the General Theological Seminary, for early Matins, Mass, and sermon on Sundays and Tuesdays, and Evensong and sermon on Wednesdays. In winter, he walked the full distance through streets deep in mud and snow. "There were fightings without," he explained, years later, "but all was peace within the blessed House of Mercy."

He was always ready to use his powers of persuasion to obtain help for the work of rescue. He knew whom to approach and how. In 1867 the New York State Legislature made them a $5,000 grant, and later gave $25,000 on a matching basis to build an infirmary-chapel addition to the old Howland mansion. The matching sum was supplied by a legacy from a Presbyterian gentleman who had heard Bishop Potter's appeal for funds in 1864.

The infirmary was desperately needed. Young as they were, many of the inmates were dying of drink, drug addiction, consumption and venereal disease. The severe limitations of medicine in 1867 are indicated in the contributions lists; there, among "bbls. turnips" and "quintals of codfish", are such medicines as spirits of hartshorn, castor oil, sulphur, cream of tartar, slippery elm and liquorice. But the new infirmary could supply such remedies as sanitation, comfort and wholesome food. One girl, Mary P., was found dying of consumption on Blackwell's Island, utterly destitute and alone. Brought to the House of Mercy, she said the clean bed was "like heaven." Another typical case was Matilda T., whose mother returned her to the House to save her from the wicked influences of her environment. The healthy and rehabilitated were sometimes sent to work in an orphanage in Iowa City, Iowa. But there were many deaths, represented in the financial reports by the undertakers' fees, itemized at an unvarying $22.

Admissions tended to include fewer professional prostitutes and more children threatened by bad environment, or sometimes, most sadly, the victims of criminal attack. To adapt to this change, the charter was amended by Act of the Legislature in May, 1869, to give as the institution's purpose

> to establish and manage an asylum or asylums for the reception and reformation of destitute and fallen women who may wish to avoid or abandon a vicious course of life, or who may be committed to said asylum for reformation by the magistrates of the City of New York.

Not surprisingly, in a nation that had jettisoned Catholic theology, a distorted notion of virtue prevailed. Chastity was equated with innocence. Having lost her innocence, a woman was "branded with the ignominious name of outcast," as a House of Mercy pamphlet said. It mattered not whether she had plunged through weakness or been pushed. Social conventions of the time required that the adulteress be scorned and the adulterer go free, as Dr. Muhlenberg charged in a fiery sermon. One result of this prevailing attitude was a traffic in "white slaves" more horrible than the Sunday Supplement writers ever devised. The House of Mercy case histories witness to the frequency with which naive girls from the country were offered jobs as domestics in brothels; sometimes they were rescued by prostitutes and sent to the House of Mercy.

The House itself was believed to be haunted. Strange sounds were heard at night, as of a heavy object being dragged across the floor. A bloody-looking stain oozed out of one wall, to the horror of everyone, including Dr. Seymour. Sister Gertrude's memoirs, dictated in 1914, recounted these mysteries, concluding matter-of-factly:

> Dr. Dix exorcised the House, and then there were no more

ghosts after that. No matter what went, nobody ever spoke about it.

On October 16, 1869, the corner stone was laid for a new addition, with Bishops Southgate, Lay and Quintard present. The new facilities enabled the Sisters to double the population of the House to eighty.

There is little doubt that one of the greatest values of the work at the House of Mercy was its role in modifying the attitude toward "fallen women." The lists of contributions began to take on a more humane note, with such games as croquet and battledore and shuttlecock among the "bbls. of bedroom china." Bishop Potter's touching reports of confirmation services at the House won even the hardest hearts among the respectable. He pointed out that even when the Sisters' efforts at the House of Mercy appeared to fail, that the Lord who was tender with the adulteress would say to them, "Nevertheless, thou didst well, that it was in thine heart to save them."

Dr. Morgan Dix, rector of Trinity Church in Manhattan from 1862 to 1908, guided the Community's first steps most wisely and tenderly, despite bigoted attacks.

The Rt. Rev. Charles Todd Quintard, Bishop of Tennessee, in academic regalia.

The Rev. Alfred Langmore, S.S.J.E., came from Cowley in 1896 to be Chaplain.

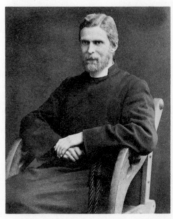

The Rev. Shirley Carter Hughson, O.H.C., was Chaplain General 1908-1918, and Chaplain of the Eastern Province 1911-1941.

The Rev. J. O. S. Huntington, O.H.C., who succeeded the Rev. William McGarvey as Chaplain of the Eastern Province in 1908.

The Rev. Charles Winfred Douglas was choir master of the Community for over forty years.

The Rev. Frank Lawrence Vernon, rector of St. Mark's, Philadelphia, Chaplain General.

CHAPTER SIX

Tribulation

UNTIL 1870 THE SISTERS seemed to be serenely oblivious of disapproval. The departure from St. Barnabas' House was amicable enough to leave no scar, and each day provided such an absorbing succession of tasks and decisions that there was little time to notice slights and suspicions. In the precious time they had together, they were busy sharing plans and problems. Slowly, their list of friends and supporters was growing, despite the generally low level of Church giving at that time. For years the House of Mercy subscribers' list was headed by "Mrs. J. J. Astor—$5."

The Sisters were increasingly conscious of the regard and affection of Bishop Potter. With no cathedral or parish of his own, he seemed to express his most heartfelt sentiments in sermons at the House of Mercy. In one such sermon he expanded on the English Reformation:

> Our Anglican fathers conducted their reformation more wisely and temperately than it was effected on the Continent. They

61

preserved the ministry and the essential order of the Church unbroken. But even in England, by a natural recoil from a body with which they were at variance, and from whose abuses they were separating themselves, they cast off not only errors and corruptions, but also some good things which they would have done well to retain. Slowly, with many alarms and convulsions, and many misrepresentations, some of the cast-off things have been gradually reclaimed by the Church, especially within the last forty years. These things reclaimed have not been Romish or mediaeval things, but things primitive and apostolic; and just in proportion as they have been recovered has the Church recovered her full life and vigor.

Some of the "alarms and convulsions" had been directed at Bishop Potter, provoked by a pastoral letter he wrote in 1865 censuring priests in his diocese for participating in joint communion services with sectarians. Though the pastoral letter was courteous and brotherly, it won for Bishop Potter the epithets "churlish and bigoted . . . overbearing and tyrannical" in the less responsible Church papers.

In 1868 he disciplined a priest so popular as a preacher that his parish, Holy Trinity at Madison Avenue and Forty-second Street, was called "Dr. Tyng's Church." This man, Stephen J. Tyng Jr., had preached in a Methodist Church in New Jersey without obtaining authorization of the parish priest there; for this offense he was tried and mildly censured by an ecclesiastical court. *The Episcopalian* attacked the Bishop for a counter-instance in which a Greek priest had said Mass in Trinity Chapel "with blazing lights and burning incense . . . the Bishop winked at it."

It wasn't long before the polemicists saw popery in the Bishop's every act. An ordination at Trinity Church was described as

a highly ritualistic affair . . . they had a processional and re-
cessional hymn composed for the occasion, and they marched,
and sang, and wheeled and performed things unknown to our
Prayer Book and usages.

The offending processional was "Holy, Holy, Holy".

Dr. Dix shared in the polemical jibes. When the General
Theological Seminary published its 1867-68 catalog with a
prayer on the front printed in the shape of a cross, *The
Episcopalian* despaired:

For an institution which has on its executive committee the
author of the popish Book of Hours, we fear there is no stopping place.

The first damaging sign of hostility toward the Sisters occurred early in 1870. A physician representing parishioners
of the Church of the Heavenly Rest approached Mother
Harriet, as she was now known, about the proposed establishment of a children's hospital. The Sisters were delighted that
their cherished dream seemed about to be realized. Six weeks
later the plan was abruptly cancelled, and funds were diverted
to another project. Sister Harriet's inquiries were met by cold
silence until, from friends, she learned that powerful persons objected to having the Sisters superintend the proposed
institution.

The fifth anniversary festival at Christ Church on February 2 was especially happy, with Dr. Dix celebrating in a
magnificent white embroidered chasuble. That afternoon,
leaving the houses in charge of the Grey Sisters, they gathered at the House of Mercy for choral Vespers and tea.

The day following, Sisters Sarah, Elizabeth, Mary and
Amelia moved the Sheltering Arms household from the
Peters mansion to a new building in Manhattanville, 129th

and Tenth Avenue. The move was made necessary by the extension of Broadway, which cut through the Peters property, taking nine of the twenty-two lots.

The new building occupied an acre and was designed to accommodate Mr. Peter's advanced theories of institutional care. The two-story brick structure provided four "cottages" for sixty children each, including separate dining room, play room, wash room and dormitory. The school was in a separate building; the children were to attend a nearby Episcopal church and in other ways to take part in the life of the community.

The Sisters' pleasure in the fine new building was dulled somewhat by their discovery that the gas had not been turned on. They found some yellow dip candles and laughed when Sister Amelia worried for fear their new neighbors would take the flickering lights for strange new ritualistic observances. Ninety children were moved, the older ones without incident on the Eighth Avenue cars. The younger ones were transported in carriages; as one load of ten babies pulled away from the old mansion, the carriage door burst open and two fell out. The frightened attendant saw the carriage wheel pass over one of them, and assumed him killed, but the child was found to have suffered no serious injury and the trip was resumed.

The Sisters waited most of Saturday afternoon for the household equipment to arrive, only to learn that the proprietor of the horsecarts had withdrawn them to another job, unnerved, perhaps, by wailing babies. At dusk, by candlelight, the Sisters improvised utensils as the little ones grew sleepier and the older children amused themselves by getting lost in the unfamiliar corridors. Their packing cases finally arrived long after dark. The next morning was chaotic as the Sisters searched for dishes, finally feeding five or six children with one cup and spoon, washing up between feedings.

On Shrove Tuesday the Sisters received from Dr. Dix a Lenten rule, admirably simple and sensible. Among other disciplines, they were to receive Holy Communion on Sunday, Tuesday, Thursday and Saturday, with silent breakfast and reading at 6:30 on Wednesday and Friday. But they soon learned that they were to have mortifications not self-imposed. No sooner had they settled in at the Sheltering Arms than they began receiving what one of them called "inquisitorial visits." These sprang from preparations and publicity for a Grand Bazaar to benefit the Sheltering Arms, to help pay for the new building. Early in March a committee of nine women descended upon both the Sheltering Arms and the House of Mercy. Invited to tour the premises, they asked minute questions, commented freely, condemned the Sisters' habit, and departed, having declined to give their names. Other inquisitors followed. Some tore beds apart for closer inspection, asked to see the condition of the children's underclothing and searched closets and cupboards for hidden crucifixes and scourges.

The Sisters found these visits wearing, and Mother Harriet sent for Sisters Teresa and Catharine to help out in the emergency. To their amusement, the neighborhood children called out to them, "Why ain't you got your hair covered?" Sister Catharine was herself Irish, and appreciated it when the Irish children nearby yelled to the children at the Sheltering Arms, "You'll never see the light of heaven, you little Protestints! All *your* Sisters know, they learned from ours!"

The evangelical cat-calls were less amusing. *The Protestant Churchman* led the charge on March 31 with a long editorial warning prospective contributors to the Sheltering Arms that the Sisters used the *Book of Hours,* which included prayers for the dead. This was followed on April 1 by a more explicit attack:

> Let us know, before the Bazaar is held, what is to be the course of the Institution in regard to this Sisterhood. We are asked for our contributions to this object. We say, in reply, that we will not contribute to an Institution which has under its management a Sisterhood, having for its Spiritual Director a man who has repudiated Protestantism. . . Our great purpose has been to strengthen the hands of the rectors of St. Bartholomew's, Grace, the Ascension, Calvary, the Atonement, St. George's, the Incarnation, the Anthon Memorial, St. Thomas', the Reformation, and the Holy Trinity in their effort to free a noble Institution from a glaring abuse, by making the disconnection of this Sisterhood the absolute condition of their cooperation.

Mr. Peters' replies to rumor and published falsehoods were not as candid as the Sisters would have preferred, but on April 1 he received a note which ended his jovial evasions. In it the rectors of five prominent parishes demanded a full investigation so that the Sisterhood, if found disloyal to the doctrines and usages of the Episcopal Church, might be asked to withdraw from the Sheltering Arms. The note was signed by the Reverends William F. Morgan of St. Thomas' Church, H. E. Montgomery of the Church of the Incarnation, Samuel Cooke of St. Bartholomew's Church, E. A. Washburn of Calvary Church, and Henry Codman Potter of Grace Church.

Mr. Peters' reaction was consistent with his intense concern for the Sheltering Arms and his relative indifference to the

Sisterhood as such. He did not arrange a tour of inspection to dispel suspicion, nor did he invite the five priests to meet with the Bishop and Dr. Dix. He simply set about quietly to find new managers for his orphanage, telling the Sisters nothing of his plan. They were surprised and hurt when their resignation was requested early in April.

The more responsible secular newspapers chivalrously defended the Sisters. The editor of the *Sun* wrote:

> The Low Church party having gained an apparent victory by driving the Sisters out of the management of the Sheltering Arms, the High Church people will not be disposed to aid the fair very liberally. Should it not prove so successful as was anticipated, the public will know on whose shoulders to lay the blame.

The editor of the *Express* wrote in Olympian detachment:

> As secular journalists we have no part or lot in the hair-splitting ecclesiastical differences which have led to this unseemly rupture—but as New Yorkers, anxious for the prosperity of a most useful and most Christian charity, we cannot but regret it; and we trust it may not, even now, be too late to so reconcile differences, as not to make them a bar to the entire success of the forthcoming enterprise. . .

The Bazaar committee rushed into print with enticing descriptions of the great fair, listing a band from the Brooklyn Navy Yard, concerts, readings and lectures, an exhibition of scientific instruments including a megalethroscope; and listing as its patronesses "the queens of society," a dazzling array of Roosevelts, Vanderbilts, Pierponts, Astors and Fishes.

The *Mercury,* a sensational weekly, devoted column after column to a gleeful description of the episode, with a seven-deck headline:

A PIOUS ROW

Fierce Onslaught on an Episcopal Institution

DR. DIX HEARING THE CONFESSIONS OF CONSECRATED SISTERS

Evangelical Ladies in the Role of Inquisitors

HIGH CHURCH, LOW CHURCH, AND NO CHURCH

&C., &C., &C., &C.,

The editor explained that the controversial *Book of Hours* contained devotions for each of the seven last hours of the Redeemer upon the cross; these devotions, he wrote, with a fine show of erudition, "are known to have been used in the tenth century."

The *Herald* took particular pleasure in describing a clerical popularity contest held in conjunction with the Bazaar. For fifty cents a ballot, one could vote for his favorite clerical dignitary, and the man with the most votes would receive a Tiffany-donated watch. When the race appeared to be a three-way draw among Pope Pius IX, Dr. Washburn of Calvary Church and Dr. Potter of Grace Church, the *Herald* editor dipped his pen in acid and wrote:

> We understand that the only objections to the Sisters were that they prayed seven times a day, and that they had Popish tendencies. We do not profess to know how many times a day the rectors of those churches (the eleven parishes named in the *Protestant Churchman*) think it safe to pray without injury to one's moral constitution. We do what praying we consider needful for ourselves, and are willing that our neighbors should enjoy the same privilege. But what puzzles us is that as soon as the sisterhood is driven out on account of their (sic)

68

Popish and praying tendencies the Pope himself should step in with a fair chance of carrying the day against the reverend gentlemen in deference to whose prejudices the expulsion of these charitable ladies was brought about. We cannot say we care much who succeeds in obtaining the watch.

Even a Philadelphia journal, the *Day,* felt obliged to comment:

It is not likely that the public will ever know why the Sisters of St. Mary were good enough to assist in establishing the Sheltering Arms, a charity in New York, without expectation of fee or reward, and not good enough to continue their labors in such good company as the rectors of eleven Episcopal churches. . . In retiring, they displayed much good sense. If they could not rule, they refused to ruin the enterprise. We rather like the Sisters of St. Mary, and whether they prostrate themselves in prayer seven or seventy times a day, takes nothing from the credit they are entitled to. . .

Unique among the comments was a letter to the *Church Journal* warning that hireling matrons had been known to deal harshly with orphans, even placing children under four in the shower bath for punishment, and adding:

Heart is required in ministering to destitute children, and if the Sisters best supply this essential quality, then let us thank God for them, oratory and serge-cloth included.

In all the words hurled in attacking and defending the Sisters, this anonymous writer alone had touched on the subject nearest their hearts.

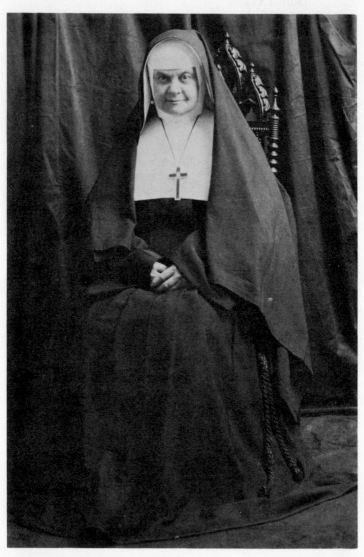

A favorite photograph of Mother Harriet, taken in her early sixties, when time had softened the strong cast of her face.

Sister Margaret Clare soon after her profession in 1883.

Sister Edith as she appeared in her years at Kemper Hall.

Kemper Hall students and Sisters shown at a ceremony for the enlarging of St. Mary's Chapel. The pierced-brass cross is still carried in the students' procession to Sunday mass.

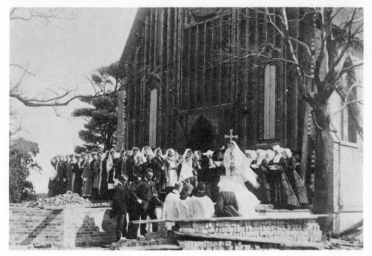

CHAPTER SEVEN

Outreach

THE DEPARTURE OF THE SISTERS from the Sheltering Arms had been saddened by the confident trust of the toddlers that the Sisters would take them along, and by the anguish of the older children, who saw their only security vanishing. Harassment and humiliation had left the Sisters utterly spent, and Mother Harriet saw clearly that they must acquire a convent in the country. Dr. Dix began searching for a suitable site; his letters at this period carried cryptic reports such as "McComb's Dam is full of fever and ague."

Their search for a country location might have been regarded as a retreat from the fray had not the Sisters first begun a new work in Manhattan which won unqualified praise in every quarter. This was the children's hospital they had so long desired, the prospect of which restored them to their accustomed gaiety. On May 19 they gathered for their first reunion since Christmas, and at breakfast after Mass, Dr. Dix entertained them with stories of his fund-collecting in Wall Street on behalf of St. Mary's Free Hospital for Children.

The Hospital was a venture as novel as it was needed. Pediatrics was a branch of medicine as yet undeveloped; most hospitals placed children in adult wards, with no provision made to supply their special needs. St. Luke's Hospital was ahead in this, as in other aspects of hospital care, but the $4 weekly charge for board was beyond the means of working people whose weekly wage was $6 or less. Moreover, children of the poor were subject to an appalling list of afflictions stemming from inadequate diet and requiring extensive treatment—spinal curvature, hip disease, deformed limbs, paralysis, club feet, weak ankles, bow legs and something called "white swelling."

By late in May, the faithful Miss Kemble had organized The Friends of the Sisters of Saint Mary to provide financial support for their several works. By autumn she had rented a house at 206 West Fortieth Street and had equipped it with fifteen beds. On September 29 the Sisters took possession, reciting Vespers in a small upstairs oratory. The next day, in a drenching rain, Mother Harriet and Sister Sarah shopped for equipment, and soon the first patients arrived.

When pleas were published for coal, cash, story books and "all bright and pleasant things", the response was most gratifying. Donations in kind were carefully listed, every glass of jelly, yard of muslin, bar of castile soap, india-rubber sheet, drum of figs and stuffed donkey. Socialites and scrub women jostle together happily in those lists, testifying to the universal appeal of sick babies. Miss McVickar's seven night gowns and Miss Van Rensselaer's fourteen bibs stand beside Dr. Dix's marriage fees and a princely $1,000 contributed by "the Hon. Wm. Tweed," the Tammany Hall boss whose graft operations were exposed the following year.

In February, 1871, Dr. Dix contributed $8,500, and the success of the Hospital was assured. Mothers who had feared to entrust their sick children to strangers now pressed for their admission to St. Mary's. The waiting list lengthened. Within two years of its opening, the premises on Fortieth Street were vacated for a larger building at 407 West Thirty-fourth Street, west of Ninth Avenue. The new quarters provided for twenty-six patients and included an adjacent lot for outdoor play. In 1873, seventy-seven patients were treated and thirteen surgical operations performed. Among these was a skull trepanation, one of St. Mary's many pioneering feats. Those were exciting days, that saw the birth of modern medicine. As a free hospital for children, St. Mary's was an ideal proving ground for new techniques. The small patients were always seriously ill, and their parents were usually willing to try any treatment, however daring. Early case records conceal in sober professional language the elation of the staff when cleft palates were corrected and hopelessly bowed legs straightened. St. Mary's became the first hospital in New York to admit acute cases. There was also heartbreaking failure and frustration, of course, most markedly in the treatment of tuberculosis. But there was success, too, in the long-term treatment of "debility," or malnutrition, and of afflictions stemming from child labor.

Without adequate medicines, doctors made do with what was at hand. Early contributions listed brandy, sherry, Madeira and rum, all of which had medical and surgical uses. Whiskey hypodermics for surgery patients were common.

The popular appeal of the Hospital was not lost on the

mass-readership press, and the Sisters now found themselves embarrassed by the effusions published in their praise. One reporter wrote:

> . . . if one wants to realize the meaning of the message 'Suffer little children to come unto me, and forbid them not, for of such is the kingdom of heaven,' let him leave the haunts of vice, the squalor of tenements, the confusion of streets, and enter this large, beautiful nursery, where reign purity and peace, and he will realize the worth and the quality of such labor given in a service of love, whose magic power in these quiet wards, bring joy and happiness as well as healing.

The Sisters' effort to discourage sentimental exaggeration elicited this comment from one daily:

> The unobtrusiveness of the Order of the Sisters of St. Mary's (sic)—their apparent disinclination to be brought before the public—undoubtedly hinders the work in which they are so deeply interested.

The Hospital work was its own reward. An old Sister, recalling the early days, could think of nothing more memorable than the promise she had received from a patient, aged four. He had assured her in a broad Irish brogue that when he became a tall policeman, and she a little, bent old Sister, he would come and take her across the street.

Soon larger quarters were required, and the Sisters decided to purchase the building they were renting and build an addition to it. The purchase alone would call for $30,000, and current operating expenses were barely met through contributions. The drive for funds opened with Dr. Dix pledging $100 a year. For ten cents and up, supporters could buy certificates in the size and shape of bricks bearing Bishop Potter's recommendation and signature. Late in February,

1876, the *New York Times* announced that 10,000 bricks had been subscribed, representing only one thirty-fifth of the total sum needed. A devastating financial depression slowed the campaign, but by autumn the Sisters purchased the building and the lot adjoining it for $27,000, of which $10,000 was paid down and $17,000 assumed in mortgage.

Early in 1878 *Harper's Weekly* carried an architect's sketch of the new hospital, an impressive five-story structure for sixty patients, to cost $70,000. The story pointed out that St. Mary's budget for 1877 had required less than $5,000 for operating expenses because the Sisters, physicians and surgeons received no pay.

The metropolitan papers carried editorial appeals for contributions and the Church press added its voice to the crusade. Even the *Churchman,* formerly so hostile, now reminded its readers that half the children who applied for admission had to be turned away.

Assured of support, the Sisters acquired a beach cottage at Far Rockaway, Long Island, for the summer care of convalescents. Within a decade of its founding, St. Mary's Hospital in Hell's Kitchen had silenced the Sisters' detractors and won a measure of peace in which they might minister to the poor.

II

Despite hard times and widespread distress, the other houses of the Community also expanded their scope in the early seventies. The House of Mercy was hit hardest by the depression, for the State withdrew financial aid just as the Sisters planned to arrange separate facilities for the older, hardened criminals and the children. This project was delayed for more than a decade, and the operating budget was halved.

The Sisters tried to decrease the annual deficit by making and selling garments; these were advertised: "For gentlemen's shirts with bosom inserted, $1; night shirts, 44¢; sac chemise, 25¢."

In March, 1871, St. Mary's School was moved from 41 West Forty-sixth Street to new quarters east of Fifth Avenue, 6 East Forty-sixth Street. There was room in the new building for one hundred students, including some thirty boarding students, and separate living facilities for the Sisters.

From the first, St. Mary's School maintained impressively high academic standards. An old account of graduation and prize day on July 2, 1874, affords a glimpse of girls' education at that time. The "salutatory" was delivered in French, followed by sixteen essays and recitations in Latin, German and English. Bishop Potter distributed prizes for proficiency in such subjects as moral philosophy, mental philosophy, rhetoric, logic, geometry, algebra, penmanship, drawing, elocution and chemistry. The prize for "deportment and lady-like conduct" went to Miss Gabrielle Greeley, whose famous father, Horace Greeley, had died tragically after his defeat in the presidential campaign of 1872.

To match external growth, the Community in the early seventies matured toward a true communal spirit. Animosity hastened the Community's development of a cohesive empathy and purpose, drawing the Sisters close in loyalty and love. A sign of spiritual maturity is seen in the eagerness with which they anticipated their long retreat in the autumn of 1870; ironically, it was this retreat which involved them in further notoriety.

Parochial duties prevented Dr. Dix from conducting their retreat and the other priests they invited declined. In mid-

November Mother Harriet learned that Father Richard M. Benson, Superior of the Society of St. John the Evangelist, had arrived at the Society's Boston House. She wrote at once asking him to conduct their retreat and he telegraphed his acceptance. Unfortunately, no one consulted Bishop Potter about the plan; when rumors reached him, he dispatched a brisk note to Mother Harriet reminding her that the English priests were not licensed to officiate in the Diocese of New York and that they would not be unless they conformed rigidly to recognized usages. Greatly distressed, Mother Harriet dispatched two Novices to Dr. Dix. They found him at his parents' home waiting for dinner, recovering from the effects of a blizzard in which his hat had blown away and he had ruined his clothing in an effort to retrieve it. Of this he said nothing to the Novices, returning with them to consult Mother Harriet. He then hurried on to see Bishop Potter. Early next morning he reported to the Sisters that he had reassured the Bishop concerning Father Benson, and had also secured his episcopal permission for the retreat as planned.

This retreat, costly as it was, marked a milestone in the Community's inner life. Father Benson at forty-six was at the height of his splendid powers. His seven meditation addresses and final sermon opened a new world to the Sisters, and at the end of the three days they were reluctant to come out of the silence.

Another sign of maturity was their true communal sense, displayed in their enjoyment of family jokes, festive worship together and holiday meals in common. They had learned to live with and laugh at misunderstanding from without and idiosyncrasies from within their ranks. Preparing for Christmas, 1870, they devised a precarious rood-screen of evergreens to hide the grimy ceiling in their oratory, and despite several lumps of pulled-out plaster, pronounced the effect most impressive. Their happiness in being a Community was emphasized for them by a holiday visit from two Sisters of St. John Baptist, Sisters Geraldine and Augusta, working alone in Baltimore far from their Sisters in Clewer, England.

III

The first step resulting from their communal maturity was a more definite formulation in 1871 of the Community ideal. By June there were nine Choir Sisters, six Choir Novices and several Postulants. The so-called Associate Sisters, or Grey Sisters, were disbanded; of the seven, Sister Anne Dana returned to Boston to become superior of the Sisterhood of St. Luke, organized by the Rev. Pelham Williams; Sister Anne Fisher's health failed; and Sister Jane Tracy entered the Choir Novitiate, becoming Sister Jane II.

Simultaneously the Community made provision for an order of Minor Sisters, for "practical duties." Adopted somewhat uncritically from European custom, the order of Minors was ostensibly for persons whose background and education did not equip them to be Choir Sisters. The Minors would perform the household work; they could not hold office, vote in Chapter, lead in Choir. They had a separate library and held recreation apart from the Choir Sisters. Their habit was blue, with the "wings" of their cornets turned down, and their ebony crosses were not bound in silver. They attended Prime, Sext, Vespers and Compline. The Community was never easy about the arrangement and nearly every General Chapter discussed abolition of the order or made changes to reduce distinctions. Of the seventeen Minor Sisters professed before the Order was dissolved in 1914, several were well educated and none fit the "servant class" designation. It was apparent that such an arrangement simply did not fit into American society.

The Community constitutions provided also for secular Associates, with no residence requirement. It was this order which developed into the splendid body of Associates whose love, prayers and alms were to prove so important to the Community's future.

The annual Chapter of November, 1871, was noteworthy for the number of monastic regulations it adopted:

A monthly chapter of discipline, for acknowledgments of breaches of the Rule.
A day of retreat each month.
Silence between noon and three o'clock each non-feast day.
Reading at breakfast on all Fridays, and every day in Advent and Lent.

The next year, 1872, the monthly chapter of discipline became a weekly chapter. All the Sisters, Novices included, seated themselves in order at the long table in the Novitiate common room and listened to the reading of the Rule. Then each in turn knelt and publicly acknowledged her breaches of the Rule, beginning with Mother Harriet and ending with the newest Novice.

In 1872 they acquired thirty acres at Peekskill, in the scenic highlands forty miles north of New York on the Hudson. Their property crowned a three-hundred-foot granite hill which had been part of the Westchester County manor granted in 1685 to the Dutch patroon Stevanus Van Cortlandt.

A clean-up crew of Sisters was dispatched to prepare the

clapboard farmhouse for use as St. Gabriel's School, scheduled to open that autumn. In later years Sister Gertrude
regaled her Sisters with tales of those first years in Peekskill.
The first summer, she said, they had so little ready cash that
a collect-on-delivery package could not be claimed for lack
of twenty-five cents. At St. Peter's Church they were regarded
with suspicion bordering on alarm. The one pew assigned
them was so crowded that Sister Gertrude was obliged to
open the pew door and extend her feet into the aisle. Their
pleas for additional pew space induced the vestry to have a
hinged board placed for them on the outside of the front
pew; during the sermon one Sunday the hinges gave way and
they were plunged to the floor.

In the autumn of 1872, the Sisters were invited to take
over the Children's Fold, at Ninety-first Street and Avenue A
in New York. The children had had such poor care that
ladies in the local parish made the ushers segregate the
orphans in the rear pews. When Sisters Gertrude and Amelia
went over to tidy up, they found the job required three
months. Mother Harriet and the Sisters finally decided it
would not be advisable for the Community to assume management of this work. Before the end of their first decade,
the Sisters did, however, acquire a new work, and re-opened
a work in Memphis begun tenuously in 1871. The new work
was Trinity Infirmary in the old Trinity Rectory in Varick
Street. The handsome six-story building at No. 50, adjoining
St. John's Chapel, was hemmed in by warehouses and tenements. The vestry of Trinity Church had long urged Dr. Dix
to move to more livable quarters, and in 1874 his forthcom-
ing marriage made a move necessary. He longed to see the
old building used for the sick poor of the parish and urged

Mother Harriet to set aside her reluctance to become involved in parochial work and undertake the project. On a bleak February day she and Sister Eleanor took over the building, now desolate of the servants and the menagerie of pets which had been Dr. Dix's only family. By April, 1874, the wards were ready and a front room had been furnished as a chapel. The day following the first Mass, the first patient arrived, a vagrant. They saw at once that he was dying, and tried to make him comfortable. After his death, they learned that he was the "prodigal son" of a minister in Maine; the father wrote them in warm appreciation that his son had died among Christian people and at peace with God. He was only the first of hundreds of derelict, diseased and drunken persons who were given the best medical care then available and often brought to the sacraments.

Even as the Community became officially involved in Trinity parish, the Sisters severed their dependence upon Dr. Dix. He had become engaged to Miss Emily Woolsey Soutter at Christmas, 1873, but for some reason had said nothing to the Sisters. Rumors reached Mother Harriet upon her return from Memphis in mid-January, 1874, but she dismissed them as idle gossip. She no doubt reproached him for subjecting her to this humiliation; in their interview of January 30, which he called "most distressing and agonizing," they apparently decided that his increased parish responsibilities and his impending domestic responsibilities would make it impossible for him to continue as their pastor. On June 3 Dr. Dix and Miss Soutter were married quietly at her mother's home, Bishop Potter officiating, and departed on a six months' wedding trip.

No one ever took Dr. Dix's place in the Sisters' affection.

81

He had run errands for them, once seriously frost-biting his face; had said a weekly Mass for them; had heard their confessions and once a month had given them instructions in the religious life. These instructions shaped the Community in a most vital way, grounding them in such fundamentals as holy obedience, temptation, work, contemplation, examination of conscience, and the order of the house. He advised the Superior and counselled the troubled. On Feasts they were invited to occupy the Rector's pew at Trinity Church, and after his annual New Year's Day reception, they received the left-over treats. He saw to their needs, shared their jokes, consulted their lawyer and inspected real estate sites. The cash books of every House recorded his benevolence, that of his wife, his parents and his brothers and sisters.

But his removal provided opportunity for growth that would have been denied had the Sisters continued to lean on his ministrations. Mother Harriet's own flowering as a superior required that she assume authority, as was pointed out to her in a letter from a priest and valued friend:

> In the Province of God you have a long time been allowed the valuable assistance of a wise head and strong hand in Dr. Dix. This was during the infancy of the Community. It must be regarded as no longer in its infancy. It must walk alone. It is old enough to do it and strong enough to do it, and it must do it. This is the meaning of your late distress. Did it never strike you as a sort of an anomaly that one actually outside a community should exercise a controlling influence within it? While your work was all concentrated in one city and every Sister under the personal direction, or at least personal influence of one priest, it was all well enough. It, in fact, was best so, but now that you are growing and stretching out your hands to distant fields of work, the real strong head must be within the order. . .

On the tenth anniversary, the Community took steps toward electing Dr. G. H. Houghton, Rector of the Church of the Transfiguration, New York, as successor to Dr. Dix. The Chapter also voted to replace the *Book of Hours* with the *Breviary Offices* translated by John Mason Neale for the Sisters of Saint Margaret, East Grinstead. In 1875, Sister Sarah, who had been Mistress of Novices since 1871, spent six months in England, sharing the training of the Novices at the Convent of the All Saints' Sisters of the Poor, Margaret Street, London. Romantic by nature and pious by inclination, Sister Sarah brought home with her many All Saints' customs, including the head-dress of starched, flaring "wings," then worn by the Sisters of the Poor.

The Sisters thus began their second decade with a new breviary, a new pastor—and a new habit.

The Sisters who died nursing yellow fever victims lie in Elmwood Cemetery in Memphis.

Old St. Mary's Cathedral in Memphis as it looked when the Sisters lived nearby.

Sister Hughetta, who survived yellow fever, became the much-loved Superior at Sewanee.

High altar at St. Mary's Cathedral, Memphis, a memorial to the Sister-nurses of 1878 epidemic.

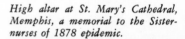

Granite was quarried from Mount St. Gabriel to provide stone for St. Mary's Chapel and St. Mary's Convent.

At the laying of the Chapel corner stone on July 2, 1890, Mother Harriet stands beside the Rev. George H. Houghton. Others, (left to right), the Rev. J. Hobart Cooke, the Rt. Rev. Charles T. Quintard, the Rev. E.F.H.J. Masse and Mr. Henry Congdon, the architect.

CHAPTER EIGHT

Planting

THE COMMUNITY HAD SENT a Sister south in 1871, when the Sisters could spare only one Novice to work there, so eager were they to help Bishop Quintard. Charles Todd Quintard and the Mother Superior were friends from Connecticut days, and had followed each other's vocations with keen interest. His medical career had taken him to Georgia and then to Memphis, where, influenced by Bishop James H. Otey, he had studied for the priesthood and been ordained in 1856. During the Civil War, he left the rectorship of the Church of the Advent, Nashville, to become Chaplain of the First Tennessee Regiment; his singular devotion earned him the honorific title "First Chaplain of the Confederacy." Like Mother Harriet, he was of Huguenot ancestry, black-eyed, magnetic, buoyant and direct. Several generals, including the fierce and formidable Braxton Bragg, were baptized by Chaplain Quintard and presented for confirmation. He was equally popular with the troops. A veteran foot-soldier commented, "W'all, when things was sort of quiet, he preached to the boys, when thar was sick and wounded, he doctored, and when the Yanks pushed us hard, he tuk a gun and fit."

Though some supposed he had "fit" himself out of all chance of being a bishop, the Church fortunately was bigger than sectional prejudice. His election was confirmed by the standing committees of the dioceses and he was consecrated Second Bishop of Tennessee in 1865. He set about energetically to rebuild his war-torn diocese. In 1867 he organized a home for war orphans; it was for help in this work that he turned to Mother Harriet.

Post-war poor as they were, the Churchmen of Tennessee within a few months raised $14,000 for the orphanage by contributions alone; Bishop Quintard forbade fairs or lotteries. By July, 1869, a building was ready on donated land in Buntyn, five miles east of Memphis. There still remained the problem of finding a suitable staff. When in 1870 a young woman from Nashville offered herself for the dedicated life in the Church, Bishop Quintard sent her to Mother Harriet in Peekskill to be trained, with the understanding that she would be returned to work in Tennessee. She had not long been clothed as Minor Sister Martha when the Bishop, pressed for help, begged for her return. The Mother yielded reluctantly, and Sister Martha took over the management of the Home from 1870 to August, 1871. Sister Martha's devotion so impressed a young society woman of Memphis that she became a Sister; she wrote of her impressions:

> I had never before been in an orphanage or any institution of the kind, and I was impressed by the utter poverty of the place and also by its order and cleanliness. On arriving the Sister took

86

me at once to her own little room. Through forty years of abiding in Religious Houses I have never seen a more perfect little cell. The whitewashed walls and the clean-scrubbed floor were spotless. Across the window was drawn a white cotton curtain. One common deal chair stood by the narrow cot with its snowy coverlid and small pillow. At the other end of the cell was a table on which was placed the Sister's Bible and Manuals of Devotion, her Crucifix and two candlesticks. Before the Crucifix was a small glass vase holding a few sweet roses. The Sister explained to me that this room was both her cell and oratory. "We have no real Chapel," she said. "The children's services are held in the schoolroom now, but when the Church is built I can say my offices before the Altar there."

Sister Martha, however, was destined to offer her worship in far more glorious surroundings. Upon her return to Peekskill for further training and profession, she became seriously ill, worn out by the year in Buntyn. She died at the House of Mercy on August 29, 1871, and was buried in the Sisters' cemetery at Peekskill.

For a time the Church Home was without a Sister, but in the autumn of 1872 Mother Harriet wrote to Bishop Quintard that the Community had decided to make a foundation in Memphis. She posed three questions, probably in the order of their importance to her:

Shall we have the privilege of a Daily Celebration?

Can the Sisters look upon you as their Spiritual Guide?

As to temporal affairs, we have no money. Can the house be secured to us free of rent for one or more years? Will any gentleman or gentlemen hold themselves responsible to make up any deficiency in our current expenses for one or more years? The school should be a "Boarding and Day School." Will a strong effort be made to secure pupils from all parts of the Diocese?

87

The Bishop's reply was apparently satisfactory, for at the Chapter in May, 1873, the Mother announced the appointment of Sister Constance as Sister Superior of the new foundation in the South. Sister Constance, then twenty-eight, was what was termed "accomplished", meaning in her case that she was a talented artist, an able teacher and linguist, and possessed of charm which "might have adorned the most brilliant social circle," according to a eulogist. Reared a Unitarian in Boston, she had overcome family opposition to be baptized and, finally, professed in holy religion. Her natural gifts were enhanced by strength of character and gifts of grace.

With such a promising Superior the Mother sent three splendid helpers. Sister Amelia had gained valuable experience working among the poor in lower Manhattan and could take charge of the Church Home; Sister Thecla, a native of Georgia recently professed, would work in the proposed school; Sister Hughetta, twenty-five, still a Novice, was a member of the eminent Snowden family in Memphis, and could help in establishing the school.

The Sisters felt the impending separation keenly, for it was to be the first time that more than forty miles had separated them. The entire Community gathered at St. Mary's Hospital to wish the four Sisters Godspeed. At Cincinnati they parted temporarily, Sister Amelia going to Nashville to visit relatives, Sister Thecla to Georgia, and Sisters Constance and Hughetta hurrying directly to Memphis.

Bishop Quintard had given over the Bishop's residence west of St. Mary's Cathedral for the new school; he and his family planned to remain year-around at their mountain home in Sewanee, where he was Vice-Chancellor of the recently re-organized University of the South. While the Sisters prepared the school and living quarters for themselves, they were guests of Sister Hughetta's brother, Colonel Robert Bogardus Snowden. The work of cleaning and renovating fell to the Sisters themselves, for their assets totalled $235, obtained by selling a watch and some jewelry. With $125 of this sum they bought a silver Communion set, leaving them $110 to open the school.

All was in readiness for classes to begin when, early in the morning of October 1, a message arrived from a Roman Catholic priest begging the Sisters to help nurse victims of yellow fever, which had broken out in his parish. Five of the Franciscan Sisters were desperately ill, Father Walsh reported, two had died, and the epidemic was spreading fast. The Sisters packed up improvised medical kits and then telegraphed Peekskill for permission to take on the nursing assignment. The Dean of St. Mary's Cathedral, their friend the Very Rev. George C. Harris, sensibly advised them to find a physician to teach them a little nursing; meanwhile, he proposed to investigate the epidemic. When Father Walsh learned from Dean Harris that the Sisters were not nurses but teachers, the Roman priest thanked them warmly but refused to let them expose themselves.

The Sisters were exposed soon after, however. As the daily deaths mounted to seventy and more, the Howard Association, a relief society of young business men, mapped the city into nursing districts, and the Sisters agreed to be responsible for the Cathedral district, adjacent to the stricken area. In all, the Sisters cared for sixty patients, of whom only eight died. Sister Amelia hurried from Nashville to take over the Church Home, where the healthy children were being moved to another orphanage. Sister Thecla joined Sisters Constance and Hughetta in setting up a relief agency in their own quarters to dispense meals to the ministering priests, as well as medicine and food to the sick. The moment a Sister appeared in the street she was besieged with pleas for help, often for shrouds.

With proper nursing, the yellow fever victim had a good chance to recover. The disease ran its course in one to five days, with headache, backache, high fever and congested face. A day or two after the onset of the fever, internal hemorrhaging began, accompanied by jaundice. At this point the victim either died or recovered, and with recovery enjoyed lifelong immunity. Not until 1881 would Carlos J. Finlay find that mosquitoes transmitted the disease. In the seventies it was believed to be spread by night air; lime and carbolic acid were spread in the streets and homes to purify the air.

Sailors infected with the virus would arrive in port, where they would be bitten by carrier mosquitoes. The 1873 epidemic began precisely in this way. Early in August a steam packet from New Orleans docked in Memphis for supplies and left behind two feverish crew members. The disease was soon spreading, slowly at first, through the Irish settlements of Pinch and Happy Hollow. By the first of September half the city's forty thousand residents had fled. Of those remaining, five thousand had yellow fever and two thousand died. The city lay paralyzed in a deadly silence, broken by an occasional mule cart loaded with coffins, rumbling down a deserted street white with lime.

The Sisters were on duty from six to six and still could not minister to all who asked their help. They omitted the recitation of Matins to perform their own housework and prepare sick rations. At seven o'clock was the Celebration of the Holy Communion. After breakfast they met with Dean Harris in the little dining room provided for his temporary use. After receiving directions for the day's work, they disinfected the house and placed squares of disinfectant-soaked linen under their clothing. Two Sisters then went on house calls, one stayed to finish housework and the other answered the bell and dispensed wine and whiskey to applicants at the door. At noon all went to the Cathedral for the Litany and noon prayers, and after dinner three went out with soup and medicine on house calls. After Vespers and tea, they relaxed, complying with Dean Harris's request that there be "no fever talk at night." They then arranged for night nurses for desperate cases, made up their accounts of expenses and donations to show Dean Harris the next day, and finally fell exhausted into bed.

Contributions poured in from many quarters, with Dr. Dix alone collecting as much as $1,400 a week, but prices had sky-rocketed and Dean Harris warned that some of the money must be saved to relieve the distress that would follow the epidemic. At times no amount of money would hire a nurse. Once the only nurse they could find was a dull girl unable to read, write or remember the doctor's orders. As the contagion mounted, the Sisters reported that their baker had died, their butcher had closed his store and begged them to come nurse his son, and their apothecary was dying. Bishop Quintard wrote encouragingly from Sewanee, Bishop Potter sent fatherly encouragement, and Dr. Dix toiled untiringly on their behalf. But when the middle of October came without the arrival of help, and when Sister Thecla appeared to be weakening under the strain, the Sisters were discouraged. That evening Sister Constance wrote to Mother Harriet:

> A pouring rain—another bad thing—it just stirs up the horrible filth of this wretched city, and leaves muddy pools to stagnate in the sun. There is no drainage—no system of cleaning the city—everyone carries the kitchen refuse into the back alley, and the pigs, which run about the streets, eat it up. I have disinfected this house thoroughly, from garret to cellar, with lime, carbolic acid, and copperas—and today the health officer came and threw tar-water all about the place—spoiling our nice clean galleries and spotting our hall carpeting in the most unnecessary manner.

If spotted carpeting offended Sister Constance's Boston sensibilities, she was comforted by one consolation:

> One comfort we have that we never had before, and perhaps could never have under any other circumstances—the Reservation—always in the Church. It is not often possible to go in, but we have the key, and it does not take long to run through the little gallery leading from the Community Room. That, and the daily Celebration, do make such a difference in our life here!

Sister Sarah, who had trained three of them in the Novitiate, wrote expressing the satisfaction of the New York Sisters to hear of the daily Celebration in Memphis,

> for in the Blessed Sacrament is our Strength—and in your needs, this Daily Bread from heaven will renew your powers to do and suffer, so that you will not fail, nor faint.

Other words of encouragement poured in, none so welcome as the notes from Dr. Dix, "our Reverend Father", as they invariably called him. He expressed his concern and spoke of waiting anxiously for the daily "all are well" telegraph dispatches. In the last week in October he reported that upon his visit to Boston the previous Sunday an offering had been taken at the Church of the Messiah for the Sisters' sick-relief fund.

By October 27, nursing demands slackened and food preparation increased, as recuperating patients regained their appetites. Sister Constance described Sister Hughetta

> getting the list of invalids' orders into portable shape—the birds into their little baskets, the soup into numerous little pails, the jelly into anything that will hold it—and we shall be busy all day in carrying things to those of the sick who cannot send for them—for you could hardly hire anyone to go into the fever-rooms, even to set down a basket. Besides, we usually have to warm the soup, & feed the patients ourselves; having by great good fortune, secured a number of the little cans of extract of beef, we usually carry some with us, and make beef-tea on the spot. Mr. Harris has grown quite used to carrying soup without spilling it, and even good old Dr. Samson has just walked off with a little bird in one hand, and a bottle of brandy in the other. I rather doubt if his patient ever sees that bird, for he is not very skillful in carrying things.

By November 1 the worst was over. Dean Harris wrote the Mother praising the Sisters'

> utter forgetfulness of self, their brave hearts shown by the steady step, unfailing readiness & cheerful faces in the worst of the dangerous work.

Bishop Quintard sent the Memphis Sisters his benediction "out of a heart penetrated with gratitude to God for giving you to me as my 'fellow-helpers' in Xt Jesus."

In her own appraisal of their experience, Sister Constance measured her phrases with Yankee economy. If the terrible year should ever be repeated, she assured the Mother, the Sisters would be equipped to be "really good fever nurses."

Imaginary scenes purporting to show socialites in retreat at Peekskill, as published in a New York daily newspaper about 1890.

St. Mary's Hospital for Children moved into this new building at Bayside, Long Island, in 1951. No child has ever been refused admission for inability to pay hospital fees.

Now devoted to convalescent and rehabilitation therapy, St. Mary's Hospital has retained and expanded its original goals of centering treatment on the special needs of children.

CHAPTER NINE

Pruning

EVEN AFTER THE EPIDEMIC and exodus of 1873, St. Mary's School in Memphis registered forty students for the year and managed to pay all expenses. With this encouragement, the Sisters enlarged the school by buying a lot on the east side of the Cathedral for $7,000, borrowed from Mr. Robert Brinkley, Colonel Snowden's father-in-law. The two houses on this property contained between them seventeen rooms, which the Sisters remodelled and refurnished during the summer of 1874. In September St. Mary's opened with eighty pupils; in addition, a nearby house became a free school for poor children, taught by an Associate, Mrs. Emma Clarke.

For the next four years, the three Sisters worked staggering schedules. Sister Constance as Superior kept the accounts, supervised the Associates, managed the academic department and taught Latin, French and history. Sister Thecla was sacristan of both the Cathedral and the school chapel, had charge of the music department, taught piano to the younger girls, managed the primary school, and taught English and Latin grammar. On Friday and Saturday afternoon she also visited the poor and sick with a companion, Mrs. Harris, the Dean's wife and an Associate. Sister Hughetta was in charge of the house, taught art, mathematics and English composition, and supervised the Guild of the Holy Child, a branch of a devotional society for school girls originated by Mother Harriet at St. Mary's, New York.

Recalling the poverty and hard work, years later, Sister Hughetta added that they lived "in a flow of charity and prayers that made life very sweet and all burdens light." The water was frozen in their pitchers on winter mornings and in summer the city lay in a steaming stench; but hardships were mitigated by the conviction that St. Mary's "was probably the best Church school in the southern states at that time." The Sisters took pride in each Commencement and recalled it as a glittering social event. Each graduate received a diploma hand-illuminated by the Sister Superior. After the Bishop's blessing there was a social hour with

> scores of white-gowned girls with huge bouquets of flowers and scores of little girls running about with the flower baskets of the seniors; of dignified fathers and happy mothers smiling upon their children, while in and out of the crowded rooms moved the stately darkey waiters carrying ice cream and cake on large silver trays—the fine trays being the property of rich and kindly neighbors.

The valedictory address of 1876, delivered by one Miss Lizzie Montgomery, was too long for publication in the local papers, but its conclusion appeared, "too beautiful to be omitted" and stands as a perfect period piece of commencement oratory:

> Schoolmates—Farewell! I fain would not have it so. What words can express my feeling for you! If the poet can say so much of the frail, soulless flowers of our parterres and fields, what does he leave me to say to you, my beautiful flowers, with germs of eternity in each heart? There is nothing more to say. To you whom in this 'rose-bud garden of girls' I have likened unto flowers, rich, rare, sweet flowers—one so pure and fair I have named a lily, another the Goddess of Flowers herself, and one in all her youthful beauty a rose, another a modest daisy, others violets and heliotropes, pinks and pansies, all buds and blossoms—may your lives be as gentle and lovely as these flowers; may no dark shadows, no heavy storms impend your pathway, so that when Death comes to call from each circle its fondly cherished one, angels may bear that soul to its God.

The Church Home, too, flourished in these five years, in part through needs arising from the yellow fever epidemic. After the first year, Sister Amelia had been obliged by frail health to surrender the direction of the Home. The Board of Trustees paid her high tribute in a resolution forwarded to the Mother Superior on October 7, 1874. By her patient labor, they said, Sister Amelia had made the Church Home "what it never was before, a clean, sweet, cheerful and home-like place." Not until 1877 was Mother Harriet able to replace Sister Amelia with another sister, the recently professed Sister Frances.

Thus the summer of 1878 saw the work in Memphis well enough established that Sisters Constance and Thecla felt able to return to Peekskill for rest and retreat at St. Mary's Convent, a three-story frame building completed in December, 1876. They had been there for two weeks when, on the

Feast of the Assumption of Our Lady, August 15, news arrived that Memphis was once again in the throes of a yellow fever epidmic. The two Sisters left at once, stopping in New York long enough to arrange for the forwarding of money and medicine. When they departed on August 17, Dr. George Houghton, Rector of the Church of the Transfiguration, stood on the steps of their carriage in front of Trinity Infirmary to give them his blessing.

Upon arriving in Memphis, they at once set about turning their residence at 352 Poplar into a dispensary. Though records show that at this point deaths averaged only ten a day, memories of 1873 had already thrown the city into a panic. By mid-August twenty thousand residents had fled. A rigid quarantine had been imposed, gangs of men had been set to cleaning the streets, and freight by rail or river from Vicksburg or New Orleans was forbidden entry. Boats from the north with such necessities as coal or coffins (ordered from Cincinnati by the thousand) were permitted to anchor in the river and unload their freight onto barges. Still the death rate mounted. The Board of Health debated the advisability of detonating fifteen kegs of powder to cleanse the air, but finally settled instead on burning one hundred kegs of pine tar. Desperate and baffled, they voted on August 29 to prohibit the importation of watermelons and ordered that fever victims be coffined and buried within six hours of death. One reads these minutes with mingled sorrow and despair. The Board members were certain that the disease had nothing to do with the open bayou which traversed the city, becoming in some places an open sewer. The suggestion that somehow the fever stemmed from "animalculae" following the course of the bayous was hooted down in derision. No, the Board decided, yellow fever was transmitted in the atmosphere, polluted by the privy vaults which honey-combed the city.

Less concerned with the cause of the disease than with its effects, the Sisters noted at once that the 1878 version was more swiftly virulent than that of 1873. The earlier fever had run its course in sixty hours; this frequently ended in horrible convulsions in twenty-eight hours. The death rate doubled by August 27 and reached seventy in one day by August 30. In house after house the Sisters found victims alone and unconscious, without medical or nursing attendance. Scraps of notes found among Sister Constance's papers after her death trace the mounting horror. By Sunday, August 25, Sister Frances was reported down with the fever at the Church Home and the other Sisters shared the night nursing with their devoted Associate, Mrs. Nannie Bullock. Sister Hughetta became ill on Monday night, August 26. It was nearly impossible to find nurses. Sister Constance wrote, "Met five or six negroes, tried to secure nurse, they said they 'were mighty jubious about this here fever', would not go."

As she answered one call, Sister Constance was met by a man who thrust a telegram into her hands and demanded that she read it. It read, "Father and mother are lying dead in the house, brother is dying, send me some help, no money." It was signed "Sallie U." Sister Constance went at once and found a pretty young girl in mourning, one corpse on the sofa, another on the bed, and a delirious, nearly naked young man rocking himself back and forth in his great agony, in an atmosphere so horrible that the Sister was sickened.

This type of scene was repeated again and again in the day's work. Five doctors had fled the city, and at times an undertaker's services could be procured only by the vexatious process of obtaining a police order. The workers were hampered in small ways, too: the horse lost all his shoes and there was no blacksmith to shoe him. Dr. Houghton sent $889, but money was fast losing its value as goods became increasingly scarce.

The Relief Association prevailed upon the Sisters to take over an orphanage for Negro children, the Canfield Asylum, and make it a reception center for all fever orphans without distinction of race or religion. Since the Asylum was in a part of the city not heavily infected, the Sisters felt justified in telegraphing Peekskill for help; in the meantime, Sister Hughetta, who had recovered from her bout of what was probably dysentery, was placed in charge. On the way to the Asylum, in a part of the city not heavily infected, she and Sister Constance were accosted by an angry mob demanding to know by what right they were bringing in children from infected areas. Sister Constance listened to their complaints and reassured them gently, finally quelling their anger with the question, "Are you not willing to trust the Sisters?" A few men mumbled, "Yes, we are," and the mob made way for the driver to proceed. The Asylum was opened next day. Within four days fifty fever orphans were received, each being bathed in carbolic solution and dressed in clean clothes before admission.

The Sisters in Peekskill were in their semi-annual long retreat when the telegram requesting help reached them. Father Grafton, the conductor, decided to end the retreat at once and return to Boston to see what the Society of St. Margaret could do to help. Of the Sisters of St. Margaret who volunteered, Sister Clare, a trained nurse from East Grinstead in England, was chosen to go. She was to meet two Sisters of Saint Mary, Sisters Ruth and Helen, in New York for the trip south. Sister Ruth, who had been called out of the retreat, wrote a brief note to her Novice Mistress, Sister Sarah:

> You will understand how gladly & unreservedly I give myself to our Beloved. The bitterness came long ago, before my Profession—there is only the sweetness now.

And to her Godmother she wrote, "Pray for me, that in life, in death, I may be ever His own."

The three Sisters left Trinity Infirmary on Saturday, August 31, and arrived in Memphis on Monday to find the Sisters there becoming dispirited and downcast. Dr. Harris had been taken ill on Saturday, and by Monday his condition was critical. Mr. Charles C. Parsons, Rector of St. Lazarus and Grace Church in Memphis, came down with the fever on Monday, leaving them without a priest. The daily deaths now exceeded eighty; four Roman Catholic priests had died, and one Sister. They felt increasingly inadequate as members of their own band fell ill. Only a few hours before he was stricken, Mr. Parsons wrote to Bishop Quintard a description of the fearful conditions, adding,

> The Sisters are doing a wonderful work. It is a surprise to see how much these quiet, brave, unshrinking daughters of the Divine Love can accomplish in efforts and results.

In their state of exhaustion, the Sisters were depressed by the panic on all hands, and by the sight of the death carts loaded with eight or nine rough pine coffins. There was the heat, the mosquitoes, the green gold flies and the wailing of the hysterical negroes. And all was worse by night when the

101

fever fires flickered and the mule-drawn death wagons rumbled by to the long-drawn cry, "Bring out your dead!"

One hopeful sign was that Sister Frances had recovered from what was assumed to be a light attack of the fever, and now Sister Clare was available to help her nurse the children in the Church Home Infirmary. Sisters Helen and Ruth went to help in the Canfield Asylum. With both priests ill, there was no longer a daily Celebration; the Sisters at the Asylum realized suddenly one evening that the day had been Sunday, but one commented, "Every day is the Lord's Day now."

On Thursday, September 5, Sisters Constance and Thecla were stricken with severe attacks of the fever. Sister Constance had spent Wednesday night watching by Mr. Harris, who showed signs of recovery. Sister Hughetta, on returning from a sick call at one o'clock Thursday afternoon, found her lying flushed with fever on a sofa in the parlor of St. Mary's, dictating acknowledgement letters to Mrs. Bullock. The two persuaded her to go to bed, but she refused a comfortable mattress, telling them, "It's the only one you have in the house, and if I have the fever you will have to burn it." They had no sooner gotten the Superior into bed than Sister Thecla came from a death-bed watch and said calmly and quietly, "I am so sorry, Sister, but I have the fever. Give me a cup of tea and then I shall go to bed." She too refused to infect the one good mattress.

By Friday morning Sister Constance was unconscious most of the time and in one lucid moment said to Sister Hughetta, "I shall never get up from my bed." That night Mr. Parsons died. Major Belton Mickle wrote,

> Some hours before his death, and while his mind was yet clear he received the announcement of his approaching dissolution

without a shock, and with the simple "trust that he had done his duty." I asked him if he had any request to make. He replied: "Take me away from here." I said, "Where do you wish to go? Will you go into the Church?" and, as if the world was fading from his view, and he beheld everything in a spiritual light, he thought of the Church, not as a building made with hands, but as the congregation of Christ's flock, and Baptism as the door of entrance, he signed himself with the sign of the cross and said, "We receive this child into the congregation of Christ's flock, and do sign him with the sign of the cross."

Mr. Parsons had faced death many times in the Civil War, never more bravely than now. He read for himself the commendatory prayer in the Office for the Visitation of the Sick and, shortly before he died at 10:30, murmured the words of the first Christian martyr, "Lord Jesus, receive my spirit." A graduate of the U.S. Military Academy, breveted a lieutenant colonel, he had commanded the Union artillery at Perryville, Kentucky in a thunderous bombardment which had been witnessed with admiration by Chaplain Quintard. After the war, while an instructor at West Point, Parsons had been present in the Church of the Holy Trinity, Brooklyn, and heard Bishop Quintard preach on repentance and the divine life. The result was his confirmation and ordination. Mr. Parsons was buried in Elmwood Cemetery, a layman, Mr. John G. Lonsdale, Jr., reading the burial office. "If his life was beautiful", wrote Major Mickle,

> his death was glorious: if, living, he would have built up a splended parish—dying, he has done more to build up and strengthen the Holy Catholic Church than any other individual of his generation.

On Saturday morning Sister Ruth received a triple blow— news of Mr. Parsons' death and the heartbreaking word from

103

Dr. William Armstrong that neither Sister Constance nor Sister Thecla was likely to survive. Without clean clothes or any help, she had put all forty children at the Asylum into wrappers. During that fearful Saturday, two more children came down with fever; Miss Waring, a nurse who had come from New York to help, was raving in delirium; the other nurse had to be dispatched to the Church Home to replace Sister Clare, who was needed to care for the sick Sisters. The city's food supply was dwindling toward famine, and even stores which still had stocks of food were closed. Sister Ruth was subsisting on soda crackers and water.

She wrote from the bedside of a feverish child at 6 p.m.,

> Dr. says Sr. Hughetta will have the fever tomorrow. Have telegraphed all to Mother. Mrs. Bullock also threatened. Sr. Helen, Sr. Clare & I the only workers now. Twelve cases at ch Home Infirmary. Howard As. Promised to send two nurses there if possible. I do try to be brave & cheerful. Another child just down with fever.

When the news of Mr. Parsons' death was published, some thirty priests from all over the nation volunteered to Bishop Quintard for duty in Memphis. The offers of non-acclimated persons were all declined, but that of the Rev. W. T. Dickinson Dalzell of Shreveport, La., was accepted. He arrived on Saturday night, to the immense relief of the Sisters. Trained physician as well as priest, wise and competent in every way, he administered Holy Communion to Sister Constance on Sunday morning. That afternoon arrived the Rev. Louis Sandford Schuyler, twenty-seven, assistant at the Church of the Holy Innocents, Hoboken, N.J. He was not acclimated, and had in fact been too frail in health to complete his Novitiate with the Society of St. John the Evangelist at Cowley,

104

but he had been in Peekskill to supply for a few days when the Memphis Sisters telegraphed that they were without a priest. He left at once for the Church of the Transfiguration in New York, where Bishop Quintard was staying, and from him received permission to proceed as far as Louisville. There he received from the Bishop word of Mr. Parson's death and permission to continue to Memphis. Dr. Dalzell was most impressed with his smile and gentle manner, but wrote,

> I asked him if he had ever seen Yellow-Fever, and if he real-ized the risk he ran in coming to Memphis. To my dismay I found that he was utterly unacclimated, and that he had come, not as many others had come, with the hope, if not assurance, that he should escape, but as the brave soldier leads the forlorn-hope knowing that all the chances are against him, but with a burning desire to help the suffering, to work while his strength lasted, and then give his life cheerfully for Christ's sake and the Church.

Sister Hughetta wrote later that Sunday, September 8, was the darkest day of all. Some two hundred new cases were re-ported, and as many deaths. She felt herself growing weak and feared she would die before Sister Constance. Late in the evening she was put to bed with a raging fever, and at mid-night heard Sister Constance in the next room exclaim "Hosanna!" again and again until her voice trailed off. It was her last word. At ten on Monday morning Sister Constance died. She was robed in her habit and carried to chapel, in her arms some white roses that Dr. Harris had received and wanted her to have. Mr. Schuyler read the burial office, and Sisters Frances, Clare and Ruth, with Mrs. Bullock, drove out in a raw drizzle to Elmwood Cemetery where Dr. Dalzell read the interment prayers. The body had to be placed in

Mrs. Bullock's family vault until the following day, for the demand for graves exceeded the diggers' ability to supply them.

In the same letter in which Sister Ruth reported these details to the Mother, she appealed for rubber sheets, old towels, a scrubbing brush, a dustpan, and *for prayers,* concluding,

> I have just whipped a big boy for tying up a goose & beating it, & filling the babies mouths with red pepper. With forty such children our hands are full.

Strengthened by the daily Celebration, now resumed, the Sisters spent the next three days working hard and adjusting to a change in the weather—the heat gave way to a cold drizzle in which the street fires from burning bedding and sickroom furniture smouldered dismally. On Tuesday, the good physician Dr. Armstrong was stricken; on the following day Sister Clare and Mrs. Bullock became ill. On Thursday, September 12, Sister Thecla entered into rest, and late in the day Mr. Schuyler was put to bed with a high fever. The remainder of the story is awful in its brevity:

On Saturday, September 14, Dr. Armstrong died.

On Monday, September 16, Mrs. Bullock died.

On Tuesday, September 17, the Rev. Mr. Schuyler died.

On the same day, a few hours later, Sister Ruth died.

On September 17, the Rev. Charles R. Huson arrived from Florida to assist; he was stricken with fever in a few days, but recovered. Sister Frances fell victim to a second attack of fever on October 1, and on October 4 died. She had labored against overwhelming odds, with twenty to thirty children desperately ill and nurses difficult to find, even at the highest wages. Nineteen of her charges died, and she went to her bed from her God-child's grave. All but four of the children at the Church Home had the fever. Sisters Clare and Hughetta recovered sufficiently to put the Home to rights.

When frost finally came, 5,150 persons were dead and Memphis itself died—the city's charter was revoked, and for many years Memphis was merely a taxing district in the State of Tennessee. High and low were taken. The toll included Dr. Paul Otey, son of the First Bishop of Tennessee; Mr. John P. Trezevant, senior warden of St. Mary's Cathedral; the Sister Alphonse, Mother Superior of St. Agnes Academy; some thirteen Roman Catholic priests and twelve Sisters and Brothers, whose deaths while nursing the sick are memorialized in Calvary Cemetery; the Rev. E. C. Slater, pastor of the First Methodist Church, whose interment was registered at St. Mary's Cathedral; and, toward the end of the plague, Jefferson Davis, Jr., only son of the President of the Confederacy, over whose body Dr. Dalzell read the burial office on October 16.

The deaths of Mr. Schuyler and the Sisters of Saint Mary elicited a flurry of newspaper publicity which is difficult to explain. Others had died unsung nursing yellow fever victims —following the epidemic of 1855 one issue of one Church paper carried obituary notices of five priests in as many dioceses, all apparently beloved pastors of bright promise. But certain worldly considerations in the '78 story appealed to the new mass readership press. Mr. Schuyler was of aristocratic background, a Roosevelt on his mother's side, and son of the Rector of Christ Church, St. Louis; moreover, he was only twenty-seven, and his personal charm made his oblation seem more poignant. The Church papers and the penny-dreadfuls vied with each other in describing the Sisters' youthfulness and accomplishments and in tracking down their family connections. They noted that Sister Ruth was the daughter of a County Judge in Newburgh; that Sister Thecla was of the Irish McMahon family that had sought refuge in France.

Tributes poured in from many sources. Col. J. B. Keating wrote, in the Howard Association report of the epidemic,

> It would be impossible to speak in too high terms of laudation of these women. . . They had won for their order an imperishable renown. . . They had proven that heroism and Christ-like self-denial are not the virtues of a particular sect.

Colonel Keating voiced a commonly mistaken idea of their vows when he added:

> They had set an example worthy of the sisterhoods of apostolic times, and had silenced those of their creed whose Protestantism blinded them to the possibilities of an order whose vows are voluntary and to be revoked at will.

The Bureau of Relief of Hartford, Connecticut wired to Bishop Quintard,

> To Sister Constance, to Sisters Thecla, Frances and Ruth, and to all who thus count not their lives dear unto them . . . we seem clearly to hear Him say: "Inasmuch as you have done it. . ."

Dr. Dromgoole saw in the epidemic the reconciliation of the sections alienated by war:

> With a lavish hand the North has soothed the fevered brow of Southern suffering . . . the demon of discord and contention has been hushed amid silent tears over the martyr's midnight grave.

Dr. James DeKoven saw the deaths of the Sisters as "giving the Sisterhood a place in the hearts of the people which cannot be shaken." This analysis seems borne out by the expressions of sympathy which poured in from many sources. A sermon preached by the Rev. John Jay Joyce in St. John's Church, Washington, D.C. on All Saints' Day, 1878, is ample evidence that in every quarter generosity, charity, and sacrifice had won friends for the religious life:

> As we read the record of these days, we hear of woman's tenderness, of woman's devotion. In every age of the Church's history we find in time of trial woman standing by the side of man, and vying with him in his work for Christ. Though the Priesthood was, for reasons, to be filled exclusively by men, yet Our Blessed Lord did not by this lower woman's privilege or woman's position, for "He was incarnate by the Holy Ghost of the Virgin Mary," and ever since the days of that Virgin Mother woman has repeated her words, "Behold the handmaid of the Lord." Early was her work organized, and made a powerful auxiliary for the propagation of the faith, by means of those quiet and gentle ministries, which are often the mightiest. And it is an indication, not a slight one, that we are getting back more and more toward primitive and Catholic methods, that we are reviving the Order of Deaconesses and instituting Sisterhoods to aid the Church's work of love and mercy. . . "The Sisters of St. Mary! God bless them," we doubt not is the thought of many a living one today, as it was the thought of many a dying one over whose last hours they ceaselessly had watched.

109

Aproned and capped children of St. Mary's Home, Chicago, on the steps of the original Home near the Cathedral, around 1900.

Mass Mound at St. Katharine's School, Davenport, erected by the Sisters in 1929 to mark the place where, in 1835, the Rev. Charles Van Quickenborne, Jesuit missionary, offered the first Mass on Iowa soil and set up a large crucifix of native walnut.

Most popular playground equipment at Ascension Parish Day School, Sierra Madre, is this great eucalyptus tree, its hollow center reached by ramp. (Far right.)

CHAPTER TEN

Mother Harriet

FOR THE LAST TWO DECADES of her life, Mother Harriet lived at St. Mary's Convent on Mount St. Gabriel, directing the slow, steady expansion of the Community and herself developing extraordinary strength and vision. In 1876, when the Sisters acquired their new frame Convent with its cupola, wide porches and jigsaw ornament, there were Sisters working in seven houses:

> St. Mary's School, Manhattan
> House of Mercy, Manhattan
> St. Mary's Hospital, Manhattan
> Trinity Infirmary, Manhattan
> St. Gabriel's School, Peekskill
> St. Mary's School, Memphis
> Church Home, Memphis

In 1896, the year of Mother Harriet's death, Sisters were working also in six new houses:

> Kemper Hall, Kenosha

St. Mary's Home, Chicago
Cathedral Mission House, Chicago
Trinity Mission House, Manhattan
Laura Franklin Hospital, Manhattan
St. Mary's-on-the-Mountain, Sewanee

In all the multitudinous tasks related to opening these houses, Mother Harriet grappled with problems, made unpopular decisions and shaped policy with little or no help from the Community's Chaplain. Greatly loved as Dr. Houghton was for his gentle goodness, he appears to have played no major role as director or adviser. He was, moreover, engrossed in the parish he had founded, "The Little Church Around the Corner", the famous appellation of the Church of the Transfiguration.

As the full weight of the Community's direction fell on Mother Harriet, the true measure of her wisdom and vision emerged. During these decades she was schooled by disappointment, suffering and sorrow, as well as by delight, joy and peace, to the perceptible flowering of her finest qualities. Incapable of duplicity or pretense, she never struck poses of mock mastery, heroics or piety. Whatever her burdens of responsibility, she lived the quiet routine and performed the small chores of the conventual life. Frequently she took on additional jobs to relieve a sick or absent Sister. At one time, serving as sacristan, bookkeeper and Novice Mistress, she reported merrily that she was monarch of all she surveyed. "Altruism," she wrote in a little notebook, "is the regard for and devotion to the rights, interests and well-being of others." Her devotion to this principle was both costly and rewarding. It cost her the surrender of her own strong will, often obstructed or deflected by her Sisters. It brought her humility

112

and sanctity. When she wrote to a Sister, "It is always better to do as another wishes than to do what oneself wishes," her words were the distillation of her experience.

In 1877 and again in 1880 the Community felt threatened by action of the General Convention. Restrictive legislation had been demanded from the early seventies. In 1872, *The Churchman* carried three long installments of "Married or Celibate Deaconesses?" by Mrs. Charles S. Peirce, who had delivered the addresses before the Ladies Missionary Relief Society of Cambridge, Massachusetts. She wrote:

> These irresponsible Sisters ruled and 'confessed' by celibate clergy that are springing up in our large cities, I think the General Convention should speedily and sharply put a stop to, by permitting no clergyman of the Church to have anything whatever to do with the direction of any establishment which does not require of every girl or woman entering them 1) the consent of their natural guardian if under twenty-five; 2) testimonials as to character and fitness, in all cases from twelve women of the parish in which the applicant was a worshipper. But my hope is, that the nobler, freer, more natural, and therefore probably more Divine order of deaconesses, as we have been considering them, will altogether sweep away and take the place of these mediaeval cloisters and their mystery-loving devotees.

Pressured by such suggestions, and others less ludicrous, the House of Bishops in 1877 passed a measure designed to "increase the efficiency" of Sisterhoods by canonical regulation. Framed in friendly terms, ostensibly aimed at "recognition," the measure was deemed hostile by the Lower House and was riddled by Dr. Dix, Dr. Seymour, Dr. DeKoven and others. As a token courtesy to the House of Bishops, the measure was referred at adjournment to a joint committee.

113

In 1880 the joint committee reported a proposed Canon on Deaconesses but proposed no legislation regarding Sisterhoods. Acting on the measure, the House of Bishops added all the restrictive legislation regarding Sisterhoods and sent it to the Deputies, intending that it supercede the joint committee report on the agenda. Dr. Dix was parliamentarian enough to point out that this procedure was out of order, that the Bishop's revision would have to go to a committee on canons while the original joint committee report was considered by the House. This was done. The Deputies passed the Canon on Deaconesses. The committee on canons reported:

> . . . Sisterhoods being voluntary organizations of Church people for Church work, and already under the jurisdiction of the Bishops and authorities of the Dioceses and parishes respectively in which their work is carried on, this House believes it unnecessary and inexpedient to legislate with respect to such Sisterhoods, and therefore it does not concur with the House of Bishops in the adoption of the Canon proposed by them. . .

In the discussion of this measure, several journalists and priests argued so vehemently against canonical control that they appeared to be claiming for religious institutes exemption from all episcopal authority. The duel of words over the Sisterhood canon made itself felt in the defeat of Dr. Dix in the 1883 election of an Associate Bishop of New York. He had been Rector of Trinity Church for twenty-one years. At fifty-six, he was still vigorous. He had a close relationship of mutual regard with the venerable Bishop Horatio Potter, whose infirmity had necessitated the election. One observer attributed his defeat to his cold reserve as contrasted with the genial affability of the man who was elected, Henry Codman

Potter. But it is surely no exaggeration to say that in a close contest, Dr. Dix's outspoken and chivalrous defense of Sisterhoods did not further his election.

When the courtly old Bishop Potter died in 1887, the Sisters assumed that his successor, Henry Codman Potter, would become their Episcopal Visitor. They somewhat thoughtlessly failed to consult him, simply alluding to the matter in a letter to him. The new Bishop Potter quickly corrected their misunderstanding in words reflecting the overstatements that had clouded the controversy on the Sisterhood canon. He implied that the Sisters could not have it both ways. They could not be both an unofficial organization of lay women and enjoy the official sanction of the Diocesan. If his logic was faultless, his attitude lacked paternal concern for Churchwomen rendering yeoman service among the poor. Magnificently *Broad* as were Bishop Henry Codman Potter's views, in the most admirable way, his limits excluded the Sisters of Saint Mary. His strong sense of social justice was applauded widely, and in 1884 he authorized the new Order of the Holy Cross for men. Toward the end of his life he countenanced certain ceremonial enrichments and appeared at Masonic gatherings in scarlet apparel with a Masonic "jewel" resplendent upon his breast. But he declined to be Visitor to the Community of Saint Mary, and his courtesies were always correct, but cold.

After Dr. Seymour was elected Bishop of Illinois, he consented to serve as Visitor. For other priestly ministrations the Sisters relied upon the Society of St. John the Evangelist. As confessors, counsellors and retreat conductors, the Cowley Fathers shaped the inner life of the Community. Father Richard M. Benson revised the Sister's Rule in 1877 and there-

115

after counselled, instructed and guided them toward a more monastic ideal. Also influential at this period was the resident Chaplain at Peekskill, Father Henry Martyn Torbert. Trained in the Cowley Novitiate, though never professed, Father Torbert encouraged the Sisters to use penances and mortifications. This mode of spirituality, though never widely adopted among the Sisters, could be traced through several generations; its spiked crosses were still to be seen in the archives after the Sisters who wore them had long since died.

II

In only one instance did Mother Harriet press her views upon the Chapter, in urging the Sisters to approve the Community's undertaking of the management of Kemper Hall. In the autumn of 1876 they received a request from the Bishop of Wisconsin to assume management of the boarding school in Kenosha, nine miles south of Racine. Their desire to accept was prompted in no small degree by the fact that Kenosha was near Racine College, directed by Dr. James DeKoven, who had won renown as a Catholic educator, and who had long been interested in the Sisters. They were, however, hard pressed, and the school appeared most unpromising. At a Chapter on November 1, 1877, Mother Harriet strongly urged them to authorize the move as "a venture of faith." She used this phrase again in a letter to the Rt. Rev. Edward Randolph Welles, Bishop of Wisconsin, adding, "If God calls, we must have no fear, but go lovingly forth in His name."

Though they did not plan to assume direction until September, 1878, the Bishop asked that two Sisters appear for the opening of the second term in February to avoid the appearance of two changes in administration. The Bishop himself planned to move into the school and superintend its affairs until the Sisters could assume its management.

Accordingly, Mother Harriet and Sister Gertrude spent a week in Kenosha early in February. A Milwaukee newspaper noted that "great sociability was manifested" at a reception in their honor, but the prospects must have seemed less than encouraging. The school had been organized as the Kenosha Female Seminary in 1865 by a group of churchmen of St. Matthew's Church under their rector, the Rev. Hugh Miller Thompson. The Hon. Charles Durkee had offered to sell them his eight-acre homestead on Lake Michigan for an annual payment to him or to his widow. The school had opened in June, 1865, as St. Clair's Hall, with Mrs. H. M. Crawford as principal. Its difficulties multiplied, and in 1867 the trustees attempted to cede over their rights and functions to the standing committee of the Diocese, which declined to accept. In 1868 the trustees composed a letter for Dr. Elmendorf to forward to "the Sisterhood in London who are founding institutions of learning in various parts of the world," as their minutes noted vaguely. In 1870, after Bishop Kemper's death, the school was in danger of falling into the hands of a Roman Catholic Sisterhood which had offered $25,000 for the property. The standing committee of the Diocese had appealed for funds to secure the title. After much manipulation and litigation, the title was secured and the school in 1870 was reorganized as a memorial to Bishop Kemper, which came to be regarded as the date of foundation.

In undertaking this work the Sisters were helping to erect a memorial worthy of the great Jackson Kemper, intrepid missionary bishop in the Middle West. He had dreamed as

117

early as 1841 of a Sisterhood, writing to his daughter Elizabeth in Philadelphia:

> The subject of a female association founded upon true Christian principles something like the deaconesses of the primitive Church is deserving of examination and would, I think, if properly presented to the members of the Church, meet with much approbation—active employment should be constantly aimed at—either in attending to the poor and sick—or in educating youths. Suppose you get from the library the life of Archbishop Sharpe of York and examine the plan which you will find, I think, in the second volume, for the establishment of Protestant nunneries. In fact, if you have time, I wish you would copy it off for me and send it in a letter to St. Louis.

Elizabeth dutifully copied out the entire proposal, drawn up in 1737, for instituting "Protestant Convents" in the Diocese of Durham. More than twenty years passed without Bishop Kemper acquiring a Sisterhood in his Diocese, but he still longed for the establishment of a girls' school conducted, as he said, "upon the highest and holiest principles, and in strict conformity to the doctrines and worship of our beloved Church." In 1864 he appealed through the Church papers for $3,500 to buy the Oconomowoc Seminary for Young Ladies, but the Church, bled by war, failed to respond to this modest plea.

In 1878, just eight years after Bishop Kemper's death, both his dreams were secured when Sister Sarah and one other Sister arrived in Kenosha. From a practical standpoint, Sister Sarah seemed an unlikely pioneer. She lacked the hardy qualities such a venture demanded. An early Sister described her as "a woman of exquisite refinement of character . . . to whom the new and untried ways of the West were peculiarly distasteful." In dedication and zeal, however, Sister Sarah was well chosen to lay the groundwork for a religious foundation. A colleague wrote:

> She came in the simplicity of obedience and left her indelible mark of the highest ideal of the Religious Life upon the Western Branch of the Community.

School opened that autumn with forty pupils, some of whom were unable to conceal their dismay at being enrolled in a convent school. More disconcerting was the debt, now totalling $14,591. Interest at rates from seven to ten per cent, plus the $600 annual payment to the Widow Durkee, saddled the school with expenses some $1,700 in addition to operating expenses, which had hitherto always exceeded income.

Early accounts spoke less of debt and worry, though, than of the Sisters' joy at their first Christmas. Friends had helped them furnish a small oratory on the third floor where they could say their offices. The Rev. Arthur Ritchie, Rector of the Church of the Ascension, Chicago, had interested some of his parishioners in the Sisters' work and they had contributed toward a simple wooden altar. Dr. DeKoven presented two fald stools, which were placed choir wise, and a bench for Associates facing the altar. On Christmas eve the oratory was decked with flowers. An Associate, Miss Nede Seymour, presented small brass candlesticks shaped like dragons and other candlesticks were improvised from blocks of wood. The Offices sung, the two Sisters, Miss Seymour and another Associate, Miss Florence Brown, later Sister Florence, C.S.M., crept down through the dark corridors to the school Chapel, which was feebly lighted by two kerosene lamps. At midnight Dr. Lance celebrated the Eucharist. "There was a thrill about that first Midnight Mass that promised great things for the future," one of them wrote.

On January 22, 1879, Bishop Welles and Dr. DeKoven held the service of blessing for the Sisters' oratory. It was Dr. DeKoven's last visit to Kemper Hall. In March he died at forty-eight, and the Sisters were bereft of their champion and adviser. They soon found how fortunate they were in having the help of Dr. Lance. In May four men sought to arouse the Diocesan Convention to the gravity of having Sisters manage a school chartered for management\ by a rector. Dr. Lance settled the issue most loyally and wisely. It was, he explained soothingly to Mother Harriet, "the old story of 'red tape' vs. life and work for the Church." He supported her insistence that the charter be amended to make legal provision for the Sisters' management, and this was done in the summer of 1879. That autumn Sister Sarah relinquished direction of the school to Sister Edith, who held the position for four years.

III

Mother Harriet in 1880 turned her attention to opening a new kind of work, a mission house in New York among the immigrant poor. Out of gratitude to Dr. Dix, the Sisters took over the Trinity Mission House on Morris Street, which had been initiated by the Community of St. John Baptist. The Mother expressed her doubts that the Sisters of Saint Mary were called to parish work, and insisted that this move must not be regarded as precedent for parochial ventures elsewhere. Despite their scruples, the Sisters developed the work, moving to 20 State Street, overlooking Battery Park. Here, and after 1888 at 211 Fulton Street, they lived and worked among the tenements, their program consisting principally of systematic parish visiting. Much of their work lay in helping German families, and later, Italian and Slavic ones, to settle in a strange land. German families were encouraged to worship at the German Chapel at 90 Trinity Place. All were invited to take part in the nine guilds of the Mission House. By 1900 more than four hundred families were on the Sisters' regular visiting list. Sister Catharine Vera alone made twenty-five regular visits a week, up and down interminable tenement stairways, carrying her little book of prayers into the poorest rooms, wherever there was trouble or sickness. The Mission House also offered sewing and cooking classes, an employment bureau, care for the aged, domestic training for half a dozen girls at a time, a dispensary, a library and Friday and Sunday Evensong and early Celebrations on feasts.

During the summers of 1880 and 1881, groups of children were taken to Far Rockaway for outings. In 1882 Mrs. W. K. Vanderbilt offered her mother's estate at Great River, Long Island. Here fifty to seventy boys and girls would be taken for a week's sea bathing, sun and sailing. Summers at Trinity Seaside Home also came to include outings for ailing mothers and their babies, as well as vacations for young working girls of the parish.

In the mid-eighties the Community undertook its third hospital, the Laura Franklin Free Hospital for Children at 17 East 111th Street, north of Central Park. Mr. and Mrs. Franklin Delano built the Hospital in memory of their niece Laura Franklin, who had been fatally burned. Although Mother Harriet was never able to assign enough

Sisters to the work, and although in the late eighties she pressed for withdrawal, the work remained under the Sisters' direction until 1899. The Hospital was later merged with the new Fifth Avenue Hospital.

Even less satisfactory was the Mother's attempt to send Sisters to a foreign mission. When a missionary who had served in China entered the Novitiate, Mother Harriet began to hope that she might fulfill earlier requests from the Rt. Rev. W. J. Boone to send Sisters to the Missionary Diocese of Shanghai. Her hopes were dashed. The Postulant decided she was not called to the conventual life, and missionaries in China expressed alarm at the prospect of nuns joining their enterprise. The plan was abandoned, to the Mother's disappointment.

More successful were Mother Harriet's ventures in Chicago and Sewanee. The opening of the Chicago house appears the more daring when one considers the plight of Kemper Hall in the mid-eighties. In February, 1883, Sister Edith was recalled to Peekskill to take over St. Gabriel's School. Sent to replace her was Sister Margaret Clare, a widow of mature years newly professed. The good Dr. Lance died of pneumonia in January, and the Board of Trustees chose this unpropitious moment to demand that the Sisters assume responsibility for the debt. Mother Harriet opposed any such transfer until the Trustees had paid off $10,000 of the debt, but her resistance was worn down by three years of agitation. Early in January, 1886, the Trustee, Dr. W. H. Vibbert, wrote that he planned a month's cruise to Bermuda and would be unable to attend the scheduled meeting of the Board, but voiced the opinion that the property and its problems had become a burden too heavy for the Trustees. He proposed a plan:

> I think the property should be offered to the Sisters on such terms as the trustees may deem wise to propose and will relieve them from further pecuniary responsibility. If they decline to take it, then we cannot afford to hold it, the property will have to be sold and the school given up. Stern necessity has brought us to this alternative. Either the Sisters must take it, or the property must be sold.

Thus, the transfer was made with the $15,000 floating debt still outstanding. The buildings were in disrepair; there was no adequate school equipment and no provision for recreation. The only breakwater, two hundred feet of single piling, was as matchsticks against the raging waves of Lake Michigan which chewed into the shore line at an alarming rate. Yet in the same year that the Sisters took on this financial responsibility, they also opened a house in Chicago to work among the poor.

Requests for Sisters had come from Chicago as early as 1878, when the Rt. Rev. W. E. McLaren, Bishop of Illinois, wrote to ask the Community to take over St. Luke's Hospital. A year later Bishop McLaren wrote to say that he had a donor willing to provide a house "for the uses of a Sisterhood engaged in education." Nothing came of these overtures, but early in 1885 Mother Harriet wrote to Sister Margaret Clare outlining her hopes for a Western foundation:

> Chicago is the only point in my mind at present as a desirable city for our real Western foundation—but I cannot say when we may be ready to make that foundation. I hoped to have had one or two postulants from that great city before this—but, alas! none have appeared, and we have none in our present novitiate to look forward to. I feel that we must have a school

to secure our independence but, if we had the means our-
selves to buy a house, I confess a drawing toward mission
work of all kinds in connection with the Cathedral.

The work begun in 1886 was not at the Cathedral, but at
little St. Clement's Mission on the South Side of Chicago.
Two years later the Sisters accepted the Bishop's invitation to
work in the Cathedral parish of SS. Peter and Paul. The
Sisters first lived at 12 South Peoria Street, where their guilds,
mothers' meetings and sewing classes soon outgrew their
quarters. Bishop McLaren raised funds to build new quarters
for them adjacent to the Cathedral, blessed on September 29,
1890. Here they worked so successfully that one of their
enterprises, a guild for young boys, had to be disbanded. It
became so swamped with energetic members that there were
not enough Sisters to control its activities. A decade or more
later Sisters would be approached by porters and delivery
men, asking, "Do you remember me? I was in Sister's guild
at the Cathedral."

The Mothers' Meeting, as one guild was called, was probably the most influential. Eighty to a hundred mothers gathered regularly to cut, fit, sew and quilt for the needs of their
homes and families, while Sisters cared for their small children. Each meeting closed with brief instruction, prayers and
tea.

From the first it was evident that shelter must be provided for orphans and children of ill and unemployed working women on Chicago's teeming West Side. The first shelter
was opened in 1894 with four children sent by the Humane
Society. Within six months the small frame house was bursting with children. A dilapidated duplex frame house next to
the Cathedral was purchased for $16,000, repaired for

$5,000 and made ready for occupancy in the autumn of 1895, when the children returned from a summer spent in two beach cottages in Kenosha. This was the beginning of St. Mary's Home, Chicago.

IV

In the spring of 1887 Mother Harriet visited Tennessee to select some mountain property where the Sisters could find relief from the Memphis summers. From Nashville she travelled south to Sewanee at the tip of the Cumberland plateau, where she was the guest of Mrs. Stephen Elliott, widow of the Bishop of Georgia. Her son-in-law, Dr. Francis Asbury Shoup, Professor at the University of the South, pointed out the many advantages of finding a site near the campus. So persuasive was he that Mother Harriet selected a farm two miles from the University for a Sisters' rest house, with an eye toward eventual mission work among the mountain people.

The Tennessee mountaineers were part of the some three million persons scattered through the Appalachian Mountains in eight southern states, presenting a curious and pathetic ethnic problem. They were believed to have originated with a Pennsylvania settlement of Ulstermen, who had migrated southward, with some German and English settlers, gradually spreading through the entire mountain area. Isolation and poverty kept them living in the manner of their eighteenth-century ancestors. Proud and reserved, honest and fiercely independent, brave in feud or war, they lived in windowless one-room cabins and scratched out a living on the mountain slopes or distilled corn whiskey. Few of them could read. An alarming percentage suffered from tuberculosis and scrofula.

News of the mountain property delighted the Sisters in Memphis. Sister Hughetta, Superior there since 1883, had interested her brother Colonel Snowden in expanding the facilities of St. Mary's School as a memorial to their mother, Aspasia Seraphina Imogene Bogardus Snowden. In the new memorial chapel the altar frontal was made of lace worn by Aspasia in 1824 at a ball honoring Lafayette's triumphal visit to New York. However flourishing the work in Memphis, the Sisters still needed a place for rest away from their responsibilities; they welcomed also a chance to live and work among the mountain people.

Arriving for their first summer on the farm, the Sisters learned that the mountain folk regarded *them* as the heathen. They invited their new neighbors to an all-day picnic to get acquainted, but the only guests to appear were three little boys. From them the Sisters learned that rumors were flying that the Sisters worshipped an idol. Further inquiry disclosed that the so-called idol was their large brass altar cross, which a local man had helped unpack. It was the first of many instances which demonstrated how the mountaineers had passed down the rudiments of a Biblical religion, despite illiteracy. Few were baptized. Instruction was limited to an occasional sermon by an itinerant, barely literate preacher.

Apparently, suspicion was soon disarmed, for at the dedication of St. Mary's-on-the-Mountain on the Feast of the Transfiguration, August 6, 1888, everyone was there from every cove and cabin for twenty miles.

The Hayes farm buildings, purchased for $3,000, were ideal for the Sisters' purposes. The three-story farmhouse, with cupola and splendid view, afforded ample accommodations for chapel, living quarters and guest quarters. The one-hundred-acre farm, leased from the University for ninety-nine years at a rental of $25 a year, included a number of tenant families to help with the work and produce some of the food. The farm's proximity to the University made it convenient for priests on the faculty to provide the sacraments.

Disease and poor diet contributed to the lassitude of the mountain people, however, and the Sisters found that many were unable to work. Trying to hire a crew to build a road, Sister Hughetta went to a nearby cabin and found the whole family seated under the trees, half-clothed and looking hungry. She asked the man of the house why he hadn't reported for road work, as he had promised to do. He replied, to Sister's irritation, that for the past several days he had been looking high and low for his pickaxe.

V

All the expansion afforded Mother Harriet great satisfaction. In established works, too, there was cause for gratification, especially in the flourishing development of St. Mary's Hospital. The building fund stood at $14,565 in 1880, with parishes and church schools from as far away as Florida and Iowa contributing. Bishop Horatio Potter gave handsomely and instituted "Hospital Sunday" in the Diocese as a special collection for St. Mary's and St. Luke's.

St. Mary's new building, completed in 1881, included a dispensary opening on Ninth Avenue where out-patients could be diagnosed and treated. It was soon evident that the dispensary could not handle all the patients who appeared. A bequest of Miss Grace Wilkes enabled the Sisters to enlarge the work and add a free mortuary chapel. As many as 18,000 patients applied each year to the Wilkes Dispensary, surgical cases in the morning, general cases in the afternoon, for treatment costing ten cents per prescription or dressing, or nothing for those unable to pay. Even so, the dispensary was self-supporting. Students from the College of Physicians and Surgeons received clinical experience and instruction at St. Mary's under a staff of eminent men serving without pay —Robert Watts, Francis Delafield, Thomas H. Markoe, Charles McBurney, Charles S. Bull, M. Allen Starr, Charles T. Poor and George Montague Swift.

The sterilized milk department of the Wilkes Dispensary distributed as many as 117,000 bottles of milk annually at a nominal charge or free. Demand was so heavy that the Sisters were obliged to limit the supply to children under one year.

The wards for sixty in-patients, later expanded to eighty, attracted much favorable comment. The newspapers noted the steam heat, ash woodwork, transoms of "cathedral glass" and colorful appointments. One multi-deck headline was typical:

LITTLE SUFFERERS

How they are cared for by
Saint Mary's Sisterhood

EXTENDING THE SCOPE OF A NOBLE WORK

The *Evening Post* reporter questioned a little girl skating on one skate on Thirty-fourth Street, asking her if she knew about the big hospital building. "Oh, yes," she replied quickly. "That's St. Maryses. It's pretty inside, too; it's for we; only you have to be sick to live there."

128

National magazines, too, devoted space to the new Hospital. Readers of *Harper's Young People* contributed toward the endowment of a bed in the babies' ward. Month by month the editor, Miss Fanshawe, reported the slowly rising total, listing each contribution, publishing contributors' letters and assuring her readers, "Sister Miriam is very pleased." The children reported with engaging candor the ways in which they had earned their contributions, from pulling basting threads to gargling alcohol while sick, "fifty cents at five cents a gargle," one little boy wrote with justifiable pride.

As the Hospital's reputation attracted more and more patients, it became necessary to find additional facilities for the convalescent and incurable. In 1889 the Sisters opened a country home in Peekskill for such patients, in a spacious old mansion presented by Mrs. McWalter Noyes, sister of Mrs. Jay Gould and widow of a priest who had served on the staff of the Church of St. Mary the Virgin, New York.

In 1893, a year of depression, unemployment and widespread suffering, the Hospital was fortunate in receiving a contribution of $5000 earned at a benefit party which made minor history as a glittering social event. George Boldt, guiding hand of the new Waldorf Hotel on Fifth Avenue at Thirty-third Street, needed to convince the public that hotels were respectable, even elegant enough for entertaining one's friends. To establish this image, he designated the opening as a benefit for St. Mary's Hospital, a favorite charity of Society's leading dowagers. Mrs. W. K. Vanderbilt engaged the New York Symphony Orchestra and its conductor, Walter Damrosch, to play for the guests in the interior garden court, with its fountains and flowers, white terra cotta walls, frescoes and stained glass. About 1500 guests paid $5 a ticket for dancing and dinner in the Empire dining hall, modelled after the grand salon of King Ludwig's palace in Munich. The chef, who had not yet attained to immortality as "Oscar of the Waldorf," created a fruit concoction for the occasion which was known thenceforth as "Waldorf Salad." Of New York's Four Hundred, some three hundred named as patronesses were suitably impressed by the twelve-story height of the building, its Marie Antoinette parlor and its Turkish smoking room with low divans and ancient Moorish armor. Fourteen patronesses headed by Mrs. Potter Palmer came from Chicago, serving along with some two dozen of Philadelphia's Biddles, Drexels, Peppers and Lippincotts and fifteen proper Bostonians, including Lowells, Sargents, Lawrences and Peabodys.

Grateful as the Sisters were for financial help in that year of depression, occasional benefits could not entirely remove the specter of poverty. The problem of paying the bills was in the hands of Sister Catharine. Given to the Community as a scrawny little crippled girl, Sister Catharine had become all things in Christ, astute business woman and hospital administrator, pioneer in pediatrics and thoughtful observer of medical and surgical advances, beloved colleague of New York's greatest doctors, yet remaining always holy and simple. Of her it was said that she never spent a penny carelessly. A patron who offered to donate one of Mr. Bell's new telephones discovered this when Sister Catharine wrote to say that $63 a year was rather much and "I cannot think that we would be justified in paying out so large a sum. . . There are . . . so many essentials that ought to come before conveniences." The first thing visitors noticed about her was the cape she wore to conceal the tortured contours of her bent little body; the second thing, which blotted out the first, was the twinkling eye and the Irish wit.

If Mother Harriet could have chosen, she would undoubtedly have wished to work at the Hospital. She delighted in its growing reputation. Unfortunately, she died before a scale model of St. Christopher's Ward won the gold medal at the Paris Exposition. But her last official act, a few weeks before she died, was a trip to Norwalk, Connecticut, to sign papers for the purchase of seventy acres for a summer hospital in the hilly country a mile from the Long Island Sound. Here, on a high point with green fields sloping gently away on all sides was built a substantial square brick building surrounded on front and sides by shady piazzas. She would have delighted to see the children from Hell's Kitchen convalescing and enjoying their first experience of broad fields and blue skies.

Among the improvements she did live to see was the new House of Mercy, moved in 1890 to a dignified building at Inwood, high on the heights of Manhattan's northernmost tip. She saw also the completion of St. Mary's Chapel, Peekskill, its massive walls built of great granite stones quarried on Mount St. Gabriel. Participants in the cornerstone ceremony were photographed, showing Mother Harriet as an old nun of immense dignity, with Dr. Houghton, his handsome old face radiant with good-humored kindness, and Bishop Quintard, whom she always called simply, "Charlie."

She died on Easter Sunday afternoon, 1896, having spent a Holy Week of sleeplessness and pain which she called "my Way of the Cross." Her nurse, Sister Emily, reported that her most frequent request was for "water fresh from the well." On Maundy Thursday she received Holy Communion and that night her nurse heard her say, "They are calling me."

131

She sank into drowsiness and then into semi-consciousness, but on Easter Even she received the last rites. At three on Easter afternoon the Sisters were summoned to her cell. As they knelt about her bed, she suddenly opened her eyes wide, raised her hands, and then, in an instant and without a sound, she was gone.

Her grave was marked with a tall granite cross bearing a simple inscription, the only marker in the Sisters' cemetery with an identification:

HARRIET STARR CANNON

FIRST MOTHER SUPERIOR OF THE
SISTERHOOD OF SAINT MARY

BORN MAY 7, 1823
DEPARTED ON EASTER DAY
APRIL 5, 1896

NOT AS THE WORLD GIVETH GIVE I UNTO YOU

REQUIESCAT IN PACE

In appraising Mother Harriet's achievement one can only marvel that she accomplished so much in little more than three decades. At her death ninety-one Choir Sisters and thirteen Minor Sisters had been professed, but sickness and age took their toll and there were never enough Sisters. Nor was there enough money. In 1889 she wrote of extra bills involved in the medicine and nursing for a dying Sister, "Neither the school or community have any money. I am borrowing from St. Mary's School Fund for present expenses."

On another occasion she wrote:

> I am up to my lips now, and the housekeeping Sister says we must have a bag of coffee. It will cost twenty-five dollars and I haven't a cent to pay for it. Oh, well! I'll order it. The money

will come from somewhere.

She never confused the dignity of her office with the worth of her person. Whatever her failings, she possessed that utter simplicity and true humility by which saints see themselves as they are in God's sight. If her failings distressed her, she knew also what God's grace had achieved through her instrumentality; and she held these two in perfect balance. In 1888 she was presented with an abbatial seal ring designed by the Rev. John Henry Hopkins, Jr. The great amethyst was incised with a lily and two stars representing Christ, the "Bright and Morning Star," and Mary, the "Star of the Sea." Dr. Dix asked if he might present it. Mother Harriet wore it at all times, and the mammoth ring is still worn by the Mother General of the Community on all official occasions.

Bits of the Mother's letters illumine her character, for she wrote with a consistent candor:

> I have written about the Breakwater. I find it hard to advise. I seem so ignorant.

> I hope the sun is shining everywhere at Kemper Hall this Christmas and in every corner of everyone's heart.

> I have just been made very happy over a letter from Sister X; it was altogether voluntary on her part . . . it was all one could desire from a Sister who means to try her best to overcome all that is evil. . . I feel I can safely trust her to you for the Mission work in Chicago. Give her a loving welcome, try to gain her love, and I think all will be well. . . You know, Dr. Pusey says, 'Our life is made up of new beginnings.'

> Try to excuse in others as far as possible what seems to you so wrong; try to think more is said than is really meant, and above all, offer the particular thing, or word, or conversation to God, ask of Him to show you what He would have you do.

Sometimes it is better to be perfectly silent, but there may be times when one should speak out plainly and fully just how it all looked to one. If there was anyone to take your place I would make a change, but at present there is no one. I do wish very much in some way that the Sister should know exactly how you feel, but she ought to hear from you, and not from any other one. Now, dear Sister, have I helped you in any way? Perhaps not, but you will see that I have tried to do so.

In a small notebook Mother Harriet wrote a paragraph which perfectly expressed her concept of authority and her devotion to freedom:

A person who has to manage others in the midst of conflicts must be endowed with great self-possession, freedom from passion and strength to resist the bias of her own mind, or rather heart; must have calm superiority which only consummate virtue can give; must never have a pre-determination, never an obstinate adherence to her own opinion, a spirit of conciliation always ready to open a door to any arrangement of matters in dispute.

The meditation notes she prepared for the Novices or for Community retreats bear the imprint of profound wisdom and insight. In one meditation she alluded to her ideals: of exclusion without loss, of oneness of aim without narrowness, of oneness of vision without blindness and of a childlike mind without childish understanding. An alumna of St. Gabriel's School paid her high tribute, recalling that the Mother had entered enthusiastically into a youthful building project:

She it was who proposed that a corner stone be laid, was present at the ceremony, signing her name to the legal looking document, and putting in the box some money, that all might be done in a proper and approved manner.

134

She bore with faults and failings. She rarely or never set herself to gain affection. Most of the Sisters loved her, but some thought her weak and worldly; frank dislike surprised her little and appeared to trouble her not at all. She herself was unfailingly kind and considerate of the needs of those around her. She had no wish to cast all the Sisters in the same mold and enjoyed their individuality of mind and manners. Likewise, in going from house to house, she enjoyed the slight variations in the mode of life and observance of the Rule. She took it for granted that the Sisters desired to keep the Rule as perfectly as possible, and she declined to stoop to suspicion or inspection. It was felt by some that Mother Harriet was too indifferent to certain religious conventions, such as marks of deference to herself; this was said to be a "source of grief" to Sister Sarah. But Mother Harriet was too much of a fundamentalist to worry about trifles, and the fundamental in every case was charity. She wrote:

> In every house there is someone who tries the Sisters especially; not one house have we without some such difficulty. Sometimes the faults are want of refinement, sometimes one thing, sometimes another. We must remember how the Lord bore with his ignorant disciples, with whom he was constantly associated; and when he was telling them of the cruel death awaiting him, they strove together as to who should be greatest, and at the very last he suffered Judas to sit at his right hand. It is this very rubbing in a Religious Order, which used faithfully works out the perfection of each member and of the Order as a whole.

And again:

> Learn to think kindly that you may learn to speak kindly. When you jest at the children's faults, remember that you are in truth amusing yourself with the failings of your inferiors.

135

Her instinctive decisions were shrewd, sound and eminently incarnational. At times she was literally "ill-advised." In one instance, when she would have followed her Lord's example by accepting a "penitent" into the Novitiate, she was advised by Father Benson not to do so on the somewhat flimsy pretext that it was better to safeguard "the purity of the ideal."

She could take a strong stand, as the following excerpt shows, but she assented, on principle, to the direction of others. When she found it necessary to give commands, they were unmistakable:

> I wish to say in regard to the whipping of children, it cannot be tolerated in any house of which we have the care. Please say to Sister X that such a thing is not permitted in this Community.

The tributes published after her death in many cases could have been paid to any holy woman, but one of her Sisters expressed in verse the essence of Mother Harriet's greatness:

> We pray thee leave us as thy last bequest
> The mantle of thy holy life of grace;
> The generous self-distrust, wherein we trace
> Profound simplicity of soul, expressed
> By cheerful lowliness of word and deed.

And Dr. Dix, whose book-length memoir was her only published biography, said it all in one paragraph he wrote to a Sister:

> How is she numbered with the Saints! And yet she was never despondent, nor depressed, nor ecstatic, nor illusionary.

The campus of St. Mary's School, Peekskill, affords a panoramic view of the Harbor, with the "mothball fleet" at (left), Dunderberg Mountain, the Hudson, and Bear Mountain (not shown).

Novices work and study for two years in preparation for profession, their training supervised by a Novice Mistress. Right: in the Novitiate library at St. Mary's Convent, Peekskill.

GLADYS RICE WASHBURN

Above left: *counting altar bread at Kenosha.* At right: *a class in theology at St. Mary's Convent, Kenosha.*

CHAPTER ELEVEN

Transition

THE DECADE WHICH SWEPT THE WORLD into a new century called for fundamental changes. As the older Sisters died, it became necessary to codify the Community rules, ceremonies, customs and constitutions for future generations. Moreover, changes in ecclesiastical thought permitted a fuller expression of Catholic life than had hitherto been advisable. Catholic worship and discipline had displaced much of the mild "High Church-ism" of forty years before, and militant Calvinism had disappeared, as one editor exulted, like "an iceberg in the Gulf Stream." The Community, it must be said, was fond of old ways, and caution combined with conservatism to oppose change. Twelve years of patient effort were required to yield formularies truly expressing the original objectives and the Community spirit; to spell out and systematize customs and traditions and couch them at last in traditional Benedictine terms.

The move forward was glacially slow at first. When

Mother Harriet died in 1896 the Community acted to fore-stall change by electing Sister Sarah as her successor. Vener-ated as one of the founding five, beloved Novice Mistress until 1890 and Assistant Superior from the first, she was a woman of unswerving integrity, in whose soul "there dwelt habitually the spirit of silent reverence and recollection." Sadly, the Sisters soon saw that Mother Sarah lacked admin-istrative capacities. The Assistant Superior who might have helped her expedite pressing matters was not named for a year and a half. The result of this would have been disastrous had it not been for the quiet, loyal assistance of Sister Edith, Novice Mistress.

Fortunate also was the arrival of a new Chaplain, the Rev. Alfred Langmore, S.S.J.E. Sister Margaret Clare on a trip to England in August, 1896, negotiated with all the delicacy of a seasoned diplomat for the appointment of a Cowley father to the Chaplaincy. With her characteristic vision and vigor, she outlined the Community's great need of organization and discipline, of an amended constitution, of a proper convent and of instruction for the young, and reminded the Father Superior somewhat hyperbolically, "Our Rule was drawn up by your Founder. And will you pardon me if I say, you began a good work in America, will you see it fail?" When arrangements seemed completed, Mother Sarah boggled at Father Langmore's youth—he was thirty-seven years old and had been professed only one year—and decreed that he be named Assistant Chaplain "to our dear Dr. Houghton," whereupon S.S.J.E. withdrew the offer. By October the diffi-culty was overcome, and Father Langmore assumed the full title and responsibility for five years. He found the Com-munity at low ebb. For twenty years Dr. Houghton had been prevented by his multiple responsibilities from doing more than hearing confessions in the eastern houses. Father Langmore set about unflinchingly to supply the needs of the Community. His fortnightly visits to all the eastern houses included regular instruction on the religious life, Church history, Bible and liturgics. He prepared a revision of the Rule, retaining the simplicity of the original Rule but improving it by the experience of the English communities. His sanity and sanctity, his firm faith and sweet reasonableness, won the Sisters to his teaching. Fifty years after his transfer to India there were old Sisters who still quoted Father Langmore as a final authority in controversy.

When Mother Sarah's health failed in 1899, it was Father Langmore who gently and lovingly convinced her that she must resign. At the election which followed, the Community divided between Sister Catharine and Sister Edith, between the old ways and the new. On the third ballot Sister Edith was elected, to the evident consternation of the older Sisters, to whom she appeared dangerously modern and liberal in her views. Mother Edith had come to the Community from St. Ignatius' parish in New York, where she had been instructed in the Catholic faith by the great Catholic apologist Dr. Ferdinand Ewer. Professed on September 8, 1879, she was sent the following day to take charge of Kemper Hall. In 1883 she was recalled to take over St. Gabriel's School, Peekskill. In 1890 she became Novice Mistress, a position in which her intellectual and spiritual gifts, utterly free from sentimentality, made a lasting impression on the lives of her Novices. Her election as Mother on June 8, 1899, turned her from the teaching and study she loved to less congenial administrative duty, but she set herself to the new task with courage, and accomplished heroic feats of development and expansion.

II

In any account of Mother Edith's immense influence, first place must be given to her greatest legacy—a Rule based on classical conventual traditions. She guided and goaded the Community through a fourth and final revision of its formularies—the Rule, the Constitutions, the Custumal, and the Ceremonial—along traditional monastic lines. Every change had to be hammered out in a revision committee, presented to the Chapter section by section for discussion, amendment and approval by two-thirds vote, and this not once but several times. Persuasion is necessary in a democratic organization, and Mother Edith found it necessary to speak again and again to reassure the older Sisters that she envisaged no departure from the original objectives. At the August Chapter in 1900, she explained that they were merely verbalizing the Community's unwritten rules:

> The Mother protested against the word "reform" as used by one of the Sisters. She said that the government of the Community needed development—that the changes to be made were in accordance with the mind of the Mother Foundress, and they would have met with her approval; that the Mother Foundress was progressive and she would have modified her own ideas in some respects and expanded them in others. The old Constitution was not well developed, and in consequence we had a large body of unwritten rule which from necessity, had come to have the same practical authority as the written rule. So tradition had become more forcible than usual. The committee on revision had tried to reduce this to paper, and about ninety per cent of the old rule had been incorporated into the new.

142

In all the revision proceedings, from the preliminary session of August 30, 1900, to the July Chapter of 1906 when the finishing touches were put on the formularies, and the Rule, Constitutions and Custumal were ratified by a vote of sixty-three to thirteen, Mother Edith's sagacity and statesmanship were everywhere evident. The minutes prove that the Community was well supplied with that virtue "which in saints is called perseverance and in others, obstinacy." In one early session in which thirty-seven were present, permission was sought for the Sisters to go without their cloaks in very hot weather. The clause was passed twenty-seven to ten. The term "Mass," which the Community had used from the first, was objected to, but its use was approved twenty-two to fifteen.

During the six-year period in which the formularies were in tentative use and undergoing revision at the hands of Chapter, the Community was advised in turn by three Chaplains, each of whom made a distinctive contribution. At the approach of Father Langmore's scheduled departure in the autumn of 1901, the Sisters asked Father William McGarvey to take the Chaplaincy, but he declined because of the pressure of his parochial duties at St. Elisabeth's, Philadelphia. The Rev. William Walter Webb, a professor at Nashotah House, was elected, but a year later he was named Dean of Nashotah and was obliged to resign the Chaplaincy. At Father Webb's suggestion, Father McGarvey was elected, and this time he accepted; he was installed on August 2, 1902. At forty-one he was at the height of his power, and well qualified for the post. He had good sense and unquestionable integrity. He was an able scholar and an effective teacher; his sermons, lectures and retreat addresses display that

143

combination of simplicity and profundity which springs from a deep and disciplined spiritual life.

It is reasonable to suppose that Father McGarvey had a hand in formulating the fourth and final revision of the Rule, as it was adopted by the General Chapter of 1905, which Chapter tendered him a "vote of thanks for his self-sacrificing labours on our behalf." This Rule, finally ratified with minor amendments by the General Chapter of 1906, was a vast improvement on the so-called Langmore revision. It is important to note, however, that the changes are chiefly in style and not in content. In content, the fourth Rule represented a skillful synthesis of its three predecessors:

The rule prepared by Dr. Dix _____ 1865-1877
The rule as slightly revised by Fr. Benson_____ 1877-1901
The rule prepared by Fr. Langmore_____ 1901-1906

Added to the composite were portions of the address Bishop Horatio Potter delivered at the Community's founding on February 2, 1865, and splendid paragraphs introducing each of the twenty-four chapters, brief and crystalline expositions of such subjects as poverty, humility, silence, enclosure and charity. In these, and in the few other paragraphs that were added, the words and ideas were from Holy Scripture or the Holy Rule of Saint Benedict. The style was changed from that of abrupt command, in the third person— from "Each Sister shall . . ." and "No Sister may . . ."—to a mellow and mature second person *thee* and *thou* which somehow contributes to the tone of classic spirituality. How much of this changed tone can be attributed to Father Mc-Garvey there is no way of knowing; he sat with the revision committee, but the proceedings of that committee were not kept. It is worth noting that the revised Rule bears no resemblance in content or expression to the rule of Fr. McGarvey's own Companions of the Holy Saviour, although phrases from the Companions' rule do occur in the Community Custumal.

The Community Ceremonial, translated from several monastic sources by Father McGarvey, was acclaimed at the time it appeared as the peer of any in Roman or Anglican liturgies. The Constitutions and Custumal were later found to be too detailed, requiring frequent amendment. Much of the later inadequacy of the Ceremonial stemmed from liturgical improvements in the Church at large, rather than from any inherent fault in Father McGarvey's work. His contribution was summed up by a Sister:

> He found the Community emerging from mid-Victorian High Church Anglicanism; he completed the evolution and left it on the whole in full practice of the Catholic faith and traditional monasticism, free from inhibitions or self-consciousness.

Father McGarvey's chaplaincy brought the Sisters into close association with the Companions of the Holy Saviour, which he had founded in 1891 to promote the celibate ideal among Anglican priests. With few exceptions, the Companions were impressionable young priests and seminary students who looked to Father McGarvey for leadership at a time when the Catholic movement was notably lacking in aggressive leaders. Judging from the two first-hand accounts extant, the Companions reflected both the high ideals and the severe limitations of Father McGarvey's thinking. He had been born of Irish immigrant laborers and at the age of nineteen had come under the tutelage of Dr. Henry Percival, for whom he worked for a time as a lay assistant at the Church of the Evangelists in Philadelphia. After graduation from the General Seminary he returned to become curate of

145

the same parish. In 1896 he became rector of the daughter parish of St. Elisabeth's, where he established a clerical community of Companions.

For Father McGarvey, the veil of the temple had never been rent. His was a narrow, hot-house ecclesiasticism, a "sacristianity" which blinded him to the realities of the Church's life and his position in it. From Father Hawks' and Father Hayward's accounts, one gathers that nothing was ever thought out, much less *plotted,* and that by drift rather than by design the Companions began to aim at re-casting the Church in a mold more to their liking, to give it the Italianate flourishes so notably absent from main-stream Anglicanism. With the flourishes, they desired a formula of certitude which, whether in its fundamentalist or papalist form, is always more manageable than the mobile synthesis of authority and freedom that remains the glory of Anglicanism.

The Sisters were less aware of this aspect of Father Mc-Garvey's position than has sometimes been supposed. In his official capacity he at no time expressed pro-Roman views. Outside the Community, however, there was widespread alarm over the Companions' activities, beginning as early as 1903 after the dedication of St. Mary's Convent, for which Father McGarvey had culled the old Pontificals to compile a service worthy of the occasion.

At 10 a.m. on October 21 the Sisters formally departed from the old wooden convent, followed by the girls of St. Gabriel's School in white. At the top of the hill they were met by the clergy, thirty priests in addition to the ten officiating priests and two bishops, the latter in copes and mitres attended by deacons in splendid dalmatics. Finally came the

146

Associates of the Community, sixty in all, whose gifts, along with two Sisters' legacies, had made possible the $75,000 structure. Large enough to accommodate seventy-five Sisters, built of grey granite quarried from the hill on which it stood, the massive three-story L-shaped convent stood now as the realization of many dreams. Through it the procession moved, their old friend Bishop Seymour of Springfield and Bishop Weller of Fond du Lac censing and sprinkling the rooms in turn. An old account described the scene vividly:

> The procession entered the convent singing the Miserere and passed through the house up the stairs to the infirmary and down through the guest House. On reaching the refectory, this being the largest room, a halt was made. The Sisters stood on one side, the clergy on the other, the Associates between. At one end of the room stood a table with linen cover, crucifix and candles; across it lay the great crucifix. A hymn was sung, after which the Bishop blessed the crucifix. The beautiful collects from the "Order of Service" were read and then with great ceremony Fr. Cowl raised the crucifix to the place where it is to hang.

The small Chapel within the Convent, dedicated to St. Scholastica at Father McGarvey's suggestion, was not as yet finished, and the procession went through the cloister with its low-sloping slate roof to St. Mary's Chapel. The doorposts and walls were sprinkled to the chanting of Psalm 122, and the altar anointed first with the oil of catechumens and then with the oil of chrism, and finally vested for the Mass.

The sacred ministers in the sanctuary included eight Companions of the Holy Saviour. We can only wonder if their presence influenced the tone of Dr. Dix's sermon:

> Dr. Dix spoke tenderly of the early days of the Community,

147

and likened the building of the convent to the growth of the Religious Life, out of the stony rock of indifference and apathy of forty years ago. He traced the beginnings of the first English Sisterhoods, and told of his visits to East Grinstead, to Clewer, to All Saints'. He set forth the value and the responsibility of Sisterhoods as witnesses to unchanging truth and unaltered standards of righteousness in a world given over to restlessness and unbelief and laxity. A self-centered life is of the nature of suicide. The Sixth Psalm is said daily in the choir offices to set forth the excellence of a life under rule. To the Sisters he addressed himself with all the vigor and authority of a true spiritual director, reminding them that these were his last words of counsel to them—to beware of self-congratulation, arrogance, censoriousness, criticism, class-feeling; to repress individualism and restlessness, to be loyal to the Church.

At the consecration the great bell in the belfry, inscribed with the name of Mother Harriet, rang out with joyous peals, and after the Mass the procession moved through the autumn-painted woods to pray beside the graves of Mother Harriet and the thirty Sisters at rest.

III

Like a good field general, Mother Edith deployed her troops to best advantage, withdrawing Sisters from Trinity Infirmary and the Laura Franklin Hospital against much opposition both within and outside the Community. Time proved her wisdom in taking these steps—there were then seventy-four Sisters, some of them infirm, scattered too widely in twelve different houses. Soon after her election there were signs of growth. The little parochial community of The Visitation of the Blessed Virgin Mary, at the Church of St. Mary the Virgin, New York, asked to be received into the

Community of Saint Mary. The Superior, Sister Mary Maude, had been trained and professed at Peekskill and was at once enrolled as a Choir Sister; Sister Mary Gabriel, who had taken her vows in New York, was given a year's training in the Novitiate at Peekskill. These, with others, made nine additional professed Sisters and a large Novitiate. When an appeal came in 1902 from the Bishop of Iowa for the Community to take over St. Katharine's School at Davenport, Mother Edith thought it well to undertake the work.

The work in the South was expanded, too. Early in Mother Edith's first term she saw the advisability of establishing a permanent school for mountain girls at Sewanee, and St. Mary's-on-the-Mountain came into being, with Sister Hughetta in charge.

The death on Easter Sunday, 1903, of the last of the founding five, Sister Mary, who had been in charge of the House of Mercy since Sister Jane's death in 1868, and the death two years later of Sister Gertrude Clare, Superior of St. Gabriel's School, were sad blows and imposed hard decisions on the Mother. Sister Mary's place was taken by Sister Gertrude, but not until 1907 was a Superior found for St. Gabriel's School, when Sister Mary Maude was brought back from Memphis to fill that post.

Weighed down by responsibility, with houses distant and travel difficult, it seemed to Mother Edith that the Community should be divided into several autonomous geographical provinces. Most of the support for this proposal came from the South. The Sisters in Kenosha made it clear that their petition for provincial status was submitted in deference to the wishes of the Superiors at Peekskill. As early as 1901, the Rt. Rev. Thomas Gailor, Bishop of Tennessee, wrote to

149

the Community authorities that he regarded this measure of independence necessary if the work in Tennessee was to survive. After much discussion, the General Chapter of 1903 amended the constitution to authorize the establishment of provinces, each having its own Convent, Novitiate, and Mother Superior, all under the oversight of the Mother Superior General. Following this plan, the New York houses became the Eastern Province, with a Mother Provincial and Chaplain Provincial; the houses then in the Chicago area comprised the Western Province; and the Tennessee houses became the Southern Province.

The provincial system of government was inaugurated on the Community's fortieth anniversary, February 2, 1905, when St. Mary's Convent, Kenosha, was dedicated and Sister Margaret Clare was installed as Mother Superior of the Western Province. Despite bitterly cold weather, many guests travelled to Kenosha for the ceremonies, in which seven bishops and six priests participated. To the chanting of prayers and psalms, the Rt. Rev. Isaac L. Nicholson, Bishop of Milwaukee, sprinkled the lintel and door-posts with holy water and proceeded through the Sisters' quarters, sprinkling and censing each room. Then, as the hymn "O Mother dear Jerusalem" was rung on the chimes, the procession entered St. Mary's Chapel, the Sisters followed by the resident chaplain, the Rev. F. L. Maryon, master of ceremonies; the Rev. William McGarvey and the Rev. W. W. Webb, Chaplains respectively of the Eastern and Western Provinces; the Rev. Frs. J. W. Gilman and G. E. Taylor as crucifer and thurifer, followed by the Bishops, vested in copes and mitres, the Rt. Rev. Frs. Osborne, Fawcett, Weller, Anderson, Morrison, Grafton and Nicholson.

After the dedication ceremonies at the altar, Sister Margaret Clare was presented by Mother Edith to Bishop Nicholson, who led her to her stall and conferred upon her full authority to rule the Province in accordance with Community law and customs. Sister Ella was then blessed as Assistant Superior and Sister Florence as Novice Mistress. Sister Frances was blessed by Bishop Charles P. Anderson of Chicago as Superior of the Chicago house; Sister Esther was blessed by Bishop Theodore N. Morrison of Iowa as Superior of St. Katharine's School in Davenport. Bishop Morrison preached a stirring sermon on the text, "This shall be my rest forever; here will I dwell, for I have a delight therein," concluding:

> Truly as we make much of our joy in God's House shall we bear without heartbreak or loss of faith and fervor the burden of work and anxiety we must carry for His Name's sake.

Among the children from St. Mary's Home, Chicago, brought along to serve the guests at dinner following the ceremonies was a little girl who would grow up to become a Sister of Saint Mary and who, as Mother Mary Ambrose, would bear for over thirty years "without heartbreak or loss of faith and fervor" the burdens and anxieties of Mother Superior of the Western Province.

Thus was solemnly launched, with episcopal blessing, the frail vessel of the Western Province. It comprised in 1905 only three centers of work. The "Convent" was really a corner of Kemper Hall and remained so until 1911, when the cornerstone was laid for a new Convent building. Kemper Hall was still burdened by debt. The Durkee annuity did not lapse until 1911, at which time the school had paid some $25,000 for less than nine acres. By 1913, however,

151

the floating debt had been retired, three new buildings erected, an adequate breakwater built, and the chapel enlarged, improvements totalling $287,000. Moreover, under Mother Margaret Clare's direction, the school had won for itself a lasting place in the affections of the local community.

It need scarcely be said that the woman who accomplished all this was a person of keen intellect and strong character. Born near Flint, Michigan, Mother Margaret Clare was orphaned early and left alone by the death of her only brother. The small legacy left for her support was spent preparing for a teaching career, but she had only begun to teach when she became engaged to a Detroit businessman, Heber Crane. They decided to delay their marriage until his business was established, but the Civil War intervened, and Mr. Crane induced his fiancee to marry him at once, to assure her a place in his family should he be killed. They were married in October, 1861, and she followed him to St. Louis where he helped train the recruits of the Third Michigan Cavalry. Six weeks after her arrival, in April, 1862, Lieutenant Crane died of typhoid fever. The young widow returned to Detroit and found a teaching position. She began to attend St. John's Church, where the Rev. William D. Armitage, later Bishop of Milwaukee, was rector. Following her confirmation in 1863 she spent vacations in New York, where she worked at Trinity Infirmary and won the Sisters' grateful affection for her tireless help. Over forty, she entered the Peekskill Novitiate with young women half her age, and immediately after her profession was sent to Kenosha.

She possessed that judicious penetration usually regarded as a masculine trait, and combined with it a womanliness of the highest chivalric ideal. To the Bishop of Milwaukee, she was the "strongest person in the Diocese"; to the Bishop of Iowa, "womanly and gentle, yet masterful and effective." She strove for academic ideals surpassing the finishing-school standards of the time; she built a history library of outstanding excellence, and insisted that the natural sciences be taught with laboratory techniques, even equipping the school with an observatory and telescope for the courses in astronomy. Generations of graduates were awed by her austere manner and the way she used the word "honor." Mother Margaret Clare's list of KEMPER HALL DON'TS were aphorisms in her own unmistakable style:

> Refinement consists less in what one does and says than in what one leaves undone and unsaid.
>
> Don't talk about yourself or your family affairs. It is a sign of verdancy.
>
> Don't be inquisitive with either tongue or fingers, because curiosity is wholly vulgar and common.
>
> Don't begin sentences with "Say!" Leave that to gum-chewing girls.
>
> Don't make a display of ruffles and ankles while sitting on the porch; don't sit on your spine.
>
> Don't be ungracious. If you do a favor, do it in a whole-souled way; if you receive one, accept it with honest thanks and acknowledgments. If you beat a game or excel in a lesson, don't exult.
>
> Don't be afraid to say upon occasion, "I don't know," or "I was mistaken."

A truly great educator, Mother Margaret Clare perhaps did not feel for the Community's work in Chicago the devotion she had to Kemper Hall. Even so, St. Mary's Home flourished under Sister Frances. The Home became incorporated in 1901 as St. Mary's Home for Children and Free

Dispensary for the Poor. (The second part of the title was dropped in 1921.) The first commitments from the Juvenile Court were received in 1902, and in 1903 the Home moved into the splendid new structure at 2822 Jackson Boulevard, on land given by Mr. Thomas Lowther, with $30,000 obtained by Bishop McLaren and the Church Club of the Diocese. This four-story building enlarged the Home's capacity and called for more Sisters; for a time the Community reluctantly withdrew the Sisters from the Mission House. In 1905, Bishop Anderson appealed to the Community to resume that work, and the Sisters went into residence again on September 8. For more than a decade the mission work continued. Sister Mary Wilhelmina did a splendid job among the women prisoners at the Bridewell; it was said that she could not walk down State Street without a greeting from at least one of the women who had received her kindly ministrations.

Every summer until 1922 the children of St. Mary's Home were transported to Kenosha free of charge by the Chicago and Northwestern Railroad, a move involving more than one hundred persons plus a freight car for clothing and household needs. In Kenosha the Mother Superior provided the Home with a horse and wagon with which to make daily collections of food. In 1904 the children consumed $100 worth of butter and milk a month; flour sold for $7.25 a barrel and two barrels disappeared every week. Donations were necessary, and the names of generous Kenosha families begin to appear in the acknowledgments—Simmons, Vincent, Allen, Lance, Cavanagh, Hannahs, Pennoyer, Head.

Back in Chicago in the autumn, the same begging procedure yielded their daily bread, and on one occasion provided a society portrait painter with a commission. Mrs. William G. Hibbard, an avid supporter of the work, asked her grown children to buy a new dray horse for St. Mary's Home. They had not quite fallen in with the idea when they asked Mrs. Hibbard to have her portrait painted by the Spanish portraitist Sorolla, who was then working in Chicago. Never given to ostentation, Mrs. Hibbard hesitated. Suddenly inspired, she struck a bargain; one portrait for one horse. "Sorolla," a chestnut mare, was added to the staff. The children at the Home were not entirely pleased; they wanted their beloved old gray horse back. But the drayman assured them that this *was* their old gray mare, only he had painted her chestnut, making a botched job of it on the legs, which were black.

In 1909 the Sisters purchased a building next to the Home and equipped it as a baby shelter and infirmary, a trained nurse in charge. This work was given up in 1911 for lack of funds.

In 1915 a gift of $10,000 presented by Mrs. Joseph Worthington of Washington enabled the Sisters to build St. Mary's Domestic Science School. The World War and industrialization provided so many jobs for the unskilled that Worthington House came to be used instead for a working girls' club. The year 1915 saw also the founding of St. Frances' Guild, named in honor of Sister Frances and founded by Mrs. Charles Palmerston Anderson, wife of the Bishop of Chicago. Until her death in 1948, Mrs. Anderson devoted herself to the Guild, working, advising, inspiring and sewing dresses for the St. Mary's children from patterns she had used for her own daughters. Her children recalled the day she slipped on the ice in front of her home on Prairie Avenue,

155

went to the doctor to have the broken bone set, and continued on her way to a Guild meeting.

In 1920 Judge John Barton Payne gave the Sisters a large house and twenty acres of land in Elmhurst. St. Mary's Home used this spacious country house until 1923, when the city of Elmhurst refused to admit children from the Home to the public schools. This was six years before the law was passed authorizing the use of state funds to pay the tuition of non-resident children attending public school from an orphanage. The property therefore was sold and the funds used for the Home.

From 1925 to 1930 the children of St. Mary's Home spent their summers at Doddridge Farm, Libertyville, Illinois, at the Katherine Kreigh Budd Memorial Home. In 1934 the trustees of Racine College, Racine, Wisconsin, invited the Home to use its forty-acre campus on Lake Michigan for summer camping. In 1935 the Sisters purchased the campus as a summer home, thus preserving to the use of the Church the property representing the lifetime labor of the great Dr. James DeKoven.

The third work of the Western Province at its inception was St. Katharine's School, Davenport, Iowa, where the Sisters prayed and labored for forty years, in what one Church paper truly called "an educational outpost." The school had been founded in 1884 by the Rt. Rev. William Perry, Bishop of Iowa, but it had fallen on hard days. The Sisters took over the work in 1902, and Sister Esther arrived from Peekskill in July to supervise construction of a chapel and gymnasium. The property comprised several acres overlooking the Mississippi where, legend said, the first Eucharist ever offered on Iowa soil had been celebrated in the early 1840's by a Jesuit

Father. Sister Esther, who was ecumenical fifty years before it became fashionable to be so, was always delighted when local Roman Catholics came as pilgrims to the shrine of "Mass Mound," and through this link she struck up friendships with Roman priests and prelates, including faculty members at St. Ambrose College. The School's growth crowded its facilities, and in 1923 the Sisters purchased a nearby house for a faculty residence. This was named the Marion Crandell Memorial House, in memory of a former teacher, Associate of the Community and Red Cross worker, who was the first American woman killed on active duty in World War I.

IV

The formal inauguration of the Southern Province was a two-day affair, held in the chapel of St. Mary's School, Memphis. On November 14, 1906, Sister Hannah made her profession. The following day, Sister Anne Christine was blessed by Bishop Gailor as the new Mother Superior, and she in turn presented Sister Herberta for blessing as Mistress of Novices. Father Grafton then presented Father Shirley Carter Hughson, O.H.C., for blessing as Chaplain of the Southern Province, thus forming a close tie with the Order of the Holy Cross, which had begun work at St. Andrew's near Sewanee in 1905. In his sermon, Bishop Gailor cited the establishment of the Province as a mission call for the Christian renewal of the South, and recalled the yellow fever deaths, which by this time had become a symbol for the ideal of sacrifice. No one, certainly not the Bishop, foresaw the trials which the newborn Province was to undergo in its brief life.

It was hoped that a Convent could be built in Sewanee, where the Community's work now centered, but at first the Novitiate remained at the Church Home in Memphis, the only house with adequate space. The Sisters in Memphis did their best to keep up the School, the Church Home, the sewing guild and sacristy work for the Cathedral and weekly instruction for the Associates. But as early as 1898 it had become evident that chronic lack of funds and frequent fever quarantines might require moving the work to another city. In 1902 Sister Hughetta had left her beloved Memphis and gone to Sewanee to re-open the Training School after a three-year lapse, and Sister Mary Maude was sent out from Peekskill to make one last great effort to strengthen the Memphis school.

The St. Mary's Training School was well worth the Community's best efforts. Sister Flora had devised the plan for the School in response to a plea from Bishop Quintard, who lamented the failure of the Church to Christianize the mountain people. Even his own evangelical fervor fell short, despite the fact that many a lowland parish in Tennessee dates its founding from a fiery sermon preached by Bishop Quintard in a sawmill or a saloon. Sister Flora reasoned that if the mountain girls could be taught homemaking and Christian doctrine, they would soon elevate their homes above the primitive level that prevailed. Just as the monks of the Middle Ages civilized the barbarian tribes in one generation by bringing children to live in their schools, so Sister Flora and Bishop Quintard employed the only system which would have a lasting influence. The School opened in 1896, and re-opened in 1902.

Here, for eight months of the year, twenty or more girls

aged ten to eighteen lived and studied the rudiments of what was called "a plain English education." They were inordinately proud of their uniform, blue dress with white apron and cap. Only for lack of space were applicants turned away. While few families could find the $50 to support a daughter for a year, hard work at home by the girls themselves and appeals for help through the mission leaflet kept the door open. Once, about to tell a second-year girl who had brought her little sister that there was no scholarship available, the Sister capitulated to the plea, "She can sleep with me, and she don't eat much." One girl who was in the Training School for only one year brought all twenty of her kinfolk to baptism. By 1906 the Sisters had more than three hundred godchildren on the mountain. The mountain people brought in their eggs and garden produce to exchange for clothing and household goods at the Mission Store, to which Churchmen from all over the country contributed. One dignified old man exchanged the twenty cents which a Sister paid him for some beans for the tin dishpan his wife had "always set her heart on."

On the Feast of All Saints, 1904, the Sisters prepared for fifty guests and one hundred came. Holy Baptism was administered to twenty-six children and adults; as they were leaving chapel an alumna of the Training School came hurrying up with her little baby, so the procession returned to the font. Starting out a second time, the procession was interrupted by an older couple with their two grandchildren who had left home before sunrise to come the twelve miles on foot, and everyone returned smiling to the font. Old accounts failed to say whether these delays gave the cooks time enough to double the rations.

Some of the baptismal names on St. Mary's records are a tribute to the human imagination. One mountain woman named her twelfth child "Even Dozen." A boy was named "Bishop Quintard," while one unfortunate infant boy was named "Sister Caroline." "Hugh" and "Etta" were common, along with such names as "Phronie Bee." One parent gave the baptizing priest the name "Virgin Mary", which Sister Hughetta quickly corrected to "Virginia Mary".

In 1903 the mountain men asked the Sisters to hold classes for them in reading, writing and arithmetic. One man argued persuasively:

> There's Joe Barry, he gets forty dollars a month where we get twenty and he gets it because he can figure up accounts in his little book. He came up here to the Sisters nine years ago and learned a powerful sight out of books and this has give him a chance we others haven't had.

The Sisters agreed to hold instruction classes, intending tuition to be free, but the men were proud and insisted upon paying fifty cents a month.

A widower with two small sons insisted that his oldest child, a girl, be spared to get some schooling with the Sisters, for a most touching reason:

> Susie's mother could read out right clear like, and seemed to take a powerful comfort in it, specially on the winter nights by the lamp when she couldn't sleep. She died young. She just faded and faded for a whole year and died young. She was a good woman.

Again and again, the Sisters were touched by the sweet generosity of the mountain people despite their abject poverty. One man earned ninety cents a night watching for rocks on the tracks of the mountain railroad and on this meager wage supported his wife and five little children. A woman walked for miles over mountain trails to bring the Sisters a gift, explaining:

> Sister, Matt has given me six fruit plates and I want to give two of them to you. I never have had anything before nice enough to give you.

A "parlor" to the mountain folk was a second room with a bed in which they could accommodate guests. One woman who had a two-bed "parlor" could boast that she sometimes kept half her forty grandchildren with her over Sunday.

The "coves" were hamlets built in enclosed circular valleys formed by spurs projecting out from the vast truncated plateau. There were Lost Creek Cove, Hawkins' Cove, and Crownover Cove, among many others. On the Feast of All Saints in 1906 more than one hundred persons came from Rowark Cove to the festivities. One man brought his father-in-law, a handsome, bearded old gentleman, and took him around to see the sights. He said, "See, Pa, there's the glass clock I told you about. You can look right into the works and see the wheels turning." But the old man was most interested in seeing "the little holy stable" his grandchildren had described to him. Another man brought his forty-year-old son to see the Christmas crib and reported, "Well, Sister, he said it was the prettiest sight he's ever seen—like what we read about in old times."

Mountain people of all ages responded eagerly to the sacramental life. On the great Church festivals hundreds came, many for baptism, and those already confirmed to confession and communion. In visiting the sick, a Sister found a four-year-old girl critically ill and asking to be baptized. Her mother insisted she must wait until she grew up and "got religion." When the Sister returned two weeks later, the child had died. Her mother told the story:

> Yes, Sister, she set her little heart on being Jesus' child. She give her pa and me no rest, night or day. Well, our minister come riding across this way and stopped in to have a sup and say a word. I told him about how Agnes took on so about being baptized, and he said it wasn't to be thought on. When he rose to go, she cried, "Don't doe away until you make me Christ's little child." He come back at that, and said, "Give me some water in a bowl," and he baptized her. I never did see a child so happy! The next day she died, sudden. Our minister came back yestereven, and when he heard she was dead, he cried like a woman. "I'll never say no to baptizing a child, again. They are the lambs of the flock."

The minister later was confirmed in the Church.

In June, 1908, the Southern Novitiate was transferred to Sewanee, living at the Mission House until the new Convent was ready for occupancy in February, 1909. In May, 1909, the Mission House burned to the ground one night; the Sisters were grateful that everyone escaped injury and that Sister Hughetta saved the Blessed Sacrament, though all clothing and household goods were destroyed.

While the work in Sewanee prospered, the Memphis houses drifted toward disaster. St. Mary's School was relinquished by the Sisters in 1910 and came under the able direction of two Associates, Miss Helen Loomis and Miss Mary Paoli. The Community's impending withdrawal from the Church Home impelled Mother Anne Christine to withdraw from the Community and found the Community of the Good Shepherd, which never numbered more than one Sister, herself. Keen, smiling, quickwitted, she was greatly loved in Memphis for her work at the Church Home. At her death in 1945 at the age of eighty-six, she was eulogized in many newspapers, and never better than by the testimony of one of her orphans:

> She taught me a lot, but the greatest things she ever taught me were faith in God and the power of prayer.

Her departure from the Community was a blow from which the Southern Province never recovered. The Province was dissolved in 1910, having fallen below the twelve Sisters required for provincial status, and the Sewanee house became a house of the Eastern Province.

GLADYS RICE WASHBURN

Old age is regarded by the Sisters as a means of growth and final perfecting. The infirmary Sisters take seriously their work of intercessory prayer (above).

In the cemetery at Peekskill (right) *the departed sleep in the shadow of a great granite cross for Mother Harriet inscribed "Not as the world giveth give I unto you."*

CHAPTER TWELVE

Chastisement

A NY ANALYSIS OF THE COMMUNITY'S first century must assign to the 1906 revision of the formularies prime significance for articulating an ethos toward which the Community had been groping from its inception. This aspect of the revision, seen as a positive factor, was to be over-shadowed in the minds of many by the departure of Mother Edith in 1908 to become a Roman Catholic. The scar of that devastating event was still visible a half century later, in a certain guarded attitude toward any change, a marked wariness of clerical influence, and a disinclination to mention the subject of "1908", as it came to be called. And yet it seemed necessary to air the painful topic fully if the Community were ever to understand what had happened and why, and to learn the lesson God meant to teach.

Extensive publicity devoted to the dedication of St. Mary's Convent, Peekskill, had listed as participants eight Companions of the Holy Saviour, linking the Companions with

165

the Sisters in the minds of many. Actually, only two of the Companions were influential, Father McGarvey, and Father Maurice Cowl, the Sisters' confessor and resident Chaplain, first at the House of Mercy and later on Mount St. Gabriel. Father Cowl advised Mother Edith, chided Sisters, prepared subjects for their meditations and counselled the perplexed. Able and assured, he handed down advice in a somewhat oracular manner on subjects of immense range as in a letter to Mother Edith in 1902:

> Whatever style of Altar and reredos is selected it would seem to me that it should be consistent with the best Catholic traditions of the Church and with the architecture of the present new buildings. The slab supported by columns with the vertical or tomb beneath is an ancient & Churchly style.

In several letters he alludes to blueprints for the priests' house on Mount St. Gabriel. He must have had a hand in planning the three-story, eight-bedroom stone structure, completed in 1906. Father Cowl's influence was obviously very great. When the crisis came, it was decisive.

Father McGarvey was also immensely influential, though his reputation as a Rasputin is somewhat discredited when it is seen that he opposed establishing a provincial system of government, and was overruled by Mother Edith. In a letter in 1902 he expressed the opinion that provinces would be "disastrous for the theological tone of the Community, for its spiritual regimen, and for its practical efficiency."

There is, then, no simple accounting for the decision of Mother Edith to leave all that she loved to begin life among strangers as a sixty-year-old postulant in a Roman Catholic convent. Those who witnessed the agony of her decision and read her subsequent letters never doubted her sincerity in what she called the ground of her action, "I have lost all faith in the Protestant Episcopal Church." Secondary influences surely must include ill health. She was worn out mentally and physically. Her health, always delicate, had broken during the arduous four years at Kemper Hall, and at times she was unable to use her right arm, evidently by reason of paralysis or pain. Furthermore, she had come to depend upon Father McGarvey for counsel and support. His letters repeatedly reassure her and bid her stop worrying.

In these circumstances, exaggerated reactions to the General Convention of October, 1907, gradually shook her faith. The crux of it was a resolution to amend Canon 19, to permit "the preaching of sermons or the delivery of addresses by Christian ministers, or men," duly licensed by the Bishop. It is difficult to understand how this innocuous measure came to be vilified as the "open pulpit canon." The Rt. Rev. Thomas F. Gailor, Bishop of Tennessee, saw it

> as a restrictive measure, adopted for the purpose of putting an end to the irregular use of our Churches in some dioceses for exploiting private theories of 'Christian Unity,' and fixing the authority to speak in Church in the Bishop.

There were those, nevertheless, who saw the controversial canon as a means of inducing the pro-Romanists to leave the Anglican fold. In March, 1908, Father Hughson wrote Mother Edith:

> However radically I differ from Father McGarvey in my attitude toward our Church, I have always had, and have now, confidence in his integrity and judgment, and I cannot be too thankful to him for what he has done to put the Community on the sound Catholic basis it now enjoys. . . For the past six months, or more, there has been a desire in certain quarters to

drive the men of his views to the wall. Wherever the matter has been mentioned in my presence, I have as strenuously as possible fought against any such proposition.

Rumors of Father McGarvey's impending defection, and wilder ones regarding the Community of Saint Mary, were being circulated as early as November, 1907, when the Rt. Rev. Charles C. Grafton, Bishop of Fond du Lac, wrote anxiously to Mother Edith, pointing out all the encouraging advances in the Church and bidding her be untroubled. At the bottom of this letter are some pencilled notes in Mother Edith's handwriting:

> I have heard the gossip afloat since the adj. of the Convention. It has seemed not suf. well-grounded to disturb one, and we are in no present danger of defection. I have never doubted the validity of Anglican orders; the question of Authority is *my* stumbling block, but unless God makes it plain that some other course is His will for us we shall abide where His Prov. has placed us. I am not anxious, but undoubt. we live in troublous times, and one needs to walk humbly & prayerfully with God. I thank you etc.

To this, "C. C. Fond du Lac," as he signed himself, responded with an admirable treatise on authority, ending

> For myself, I believe the Papacy to be the growth of a worldly spirit, like the desire of Israel for a King. By demanding unscriptural & uncanonical conditions for communion, it (the Roman Catholic Church) places itself in a schismatical position everywhere. The differences between it & the Eastern and Anglican Churches can only be settled by an Ecumenical Council. For any individual to assume such a power & leave our Church, is to run the risk of losing one's reward or something worse. Yours ever in the Catholic Faith. . .

In mid-January Father Cowl wrote from Philadelphia

questioning the motives of those directing anxious inquiries to the Companions, adding

> Father McGarvey is well & not worried and hopes that you and your Sisters will not be disturbed by the interference of outsiders with questionable motives.

The same day that Mother Edith received this note she wrote to Dr. F. M. Clendinin, their good friend, begging him to appeal to a mutual clerical friend to desist from writing Sisters letters reflecting upon the integrity of the Chaplain General and the Mother Superior, labeling such as "unwarrantable intrusion", and insisting

> We are loyal Churchwomen; and resent deeply what can be regarded only as meddlesomeness. Nobody is urging us to go to Rome, and we are not more likely to go there than to Lasa, or Geneva.

No denials stemmed the excitement, however, and with a fine sense of honor Father McGarvey resigned as Chaplain General on February 1, 1908, to prevent his harming the Community by his involvement with it. In March he resigned also as Chaplain Provincial. At his suggestion, the Chapter of the Eastern Province elected the Rev. J. O. S. Huntington, O. H. C., as Provincial Chaplain. Father McGarvey's last act as Chaplain General was the installation of Father Huntington on March 19.

In view of the denials, it seems strange that early in March the Sister Superior in Chicago was alarmed by reports spread by one of the Companions to the effect that several prominent Sisters of the Community were shortly departing for Romanism. Not until June did any Sisters leave. On June 10 Sister Eliza departed and on June 12 Sister Marina joined her. There was little surprise over either departure. Sister Eliza's inherited instability and poor health had been painfully evident during her five years of professed life, and Sister Marina's discontent had increased with advancing age and infirmity.

This news was doubtless relayed to Mother Edith, who was at the Seaside Home at Great River, L.I., on her rest, accompanied by a young Sister recovering from severe illness. A letter from the Mother to Sister Mary Virginia on June 21 gave no evidence of distress, but simply inquired cheerfully into affairs at the Convent and added that she hoped to return to the Convent the following Thursday. When the Mother and her companion arrived in New York, she sent the younger Sister on to Peekskill while she stayed in the city to perform "an errand." Later it was learned that she stopped at St. Mary's School in Forty-sixth Street for a conference with Father Cowl. He evidently convinced her that she must take the drastic step, and perhaps helped her plan the manner of taking it.

On Monday morning, July 6, while the Sisters were in St. Mary's Chapel reciting Terce, Mother Edith quietly left the convent, stating her intention but giving no destination in a note found in her cell. Days later newspapers from New York to Chicago set forth the meager facts, filled out with much fiction. Miss Edith Pardee, the accounts read, late superior of an Anglican convent at Peekskill, had gone to the Sisters of the Blessed Sacrament for Indians and Colored People in Cornwells Heights, Pennsylvania, near Philadelphia. Her Sisters, the accounts declared, were following, and the Fathers of St. Vincent de Paul were taking over the extensive property at Peekskill, and so on.

170

There was no panic, but everywhere signs of suffering mingled with the indignation of those Sisters who felt betrayed. Contrary to news reports, only one Sister followed Mother Edith, Sister Grace, who left on July 31.

One of the Blessed Sacrament Sisters later related how Sister Eliza was the first to come to them, how on July 7 Sister Eliza went into New York to meet Mother Edith and bring her to Cornwells Heights, and how they were met at the door by the Reverend Mother Katharine Drexel, Foundress of the Community. She continued:

> Sister M. Edith showed signs of great strain and fatigue, and was so weak that she could scarcely walk up the steps leading to the Convent. She came to us in the habit of her Anglican Order, and when she heroically laid it aside, she said with tears welling to her eyes, 'I loved it.'

Sister Eliza soon departed her new community and subsequently tried her vocation in two Roman Catholic cloistered orders, before returning to secular life.

Sister M. Edith persevered and after her profession became assistant to Mother Katharine Drexel. The Peekskill Sisters sent her a check for $100 toward the expenses of her novitiate training, a trunk full of clothing and letters and little remembrances from time to time. She in turn wrote them regularly until her last illness in 1923. Not long before her terminal illness she was appointed Superior of the Convent in Nashville, Tennessee. Her letters indicated that she found peace at last, but that she often longed for Peekskill.

> *August 4, 1908:* I have had no word from home since Friday last, and my heart is hungry to know how things have gone. But I have no *right* to know, and must be content with the

171

inevitable fact that you will, *all of you,* gradually drop me out of your hearts and lives, even though not out of your memory. . . I came away from moral necessity; not because our fathers had come, but because I could not stay.

August 15, 1908: The Companions really had nothing to do with my state of mind; the fact that they had left did, however, show me that I too could do it. But it breaks my heart to leave you all, and the dear home I so much love. I shall never see the marigolds again, nor the orchard in bloom, nor the greenhouse. I wish it had got further along so as to be sure of being finished for you. Write to me, dear Sister, and tell me how Mr. Fry is doing, about George, & Frost and old Sara. . . I am so glad you have Sr. Catharine as the Mother—if you had elected her nine years ago things might, *would* have been different, but I have tried to do right, and to give of my best, God knows.

She noted that the Blessed Sacrament Novitiate extended much more freedom to Novices, with less of military precision and more light-heartedness, with better results. But the Latin Offices never satisfied her.

February 12, 1909: I do miss the Breviary Offices, and often wish I had one (a Breviary) that I need not forget the Antiphons and hymns. We have some of the hymns—Quem terra and O Gloriosa for instance—but there are others I am loath to have pass out of my mind. I wish I had the matins hymn for H. Guardian Angels. And I miss the river and the hills. I shall never get over missing them. . .

February 1, 1919: Some day, after the poor body with its limitations is laid away, I am coming back to see you all— you may meet me in the corridor, or see me in the chapel—in the lowest place. . . I wonder if you would let me have my old Manuals. I should be so grateful for them. The prayers are about the same as those I use now, but in so much better

English! I miss the good English, and still use my King James Bible.

She died on February 7, 1923. In her obituary in *The Catholic Standard* Archbishop Ryan called her conversion "one of the greatest acts of heroism" he had ever known.

In retrospect, it was possible to see in the tragedy the over-ruling Providence of God. In deep humility Sister Catharine pondered what hardness of heart, what communal arrogance, required such a wound for cure. Three days after the blow, she wrote:

> Oh! if each one of us could only forget her own petty un-charities, trials, and desires for position, and rise up as one, we would have learned the lesson that this bitterness was meant to teach us. I feel that disloyalty and endless petty grievances were as large a factor as Church conditions in bringing this blow upon us. God help us all.

Finally, the Sisters both at Peekskill and Cornwells Heights were made acutely aware of the sinful gulf of separation between the members of Christ's Body. With only one exception, a letter from a Superior at Peekskill, the two Communities treated each other with the utmost kindness and courtesy. Throughout the Community of Saint Mary there has been since 1908 unceasing prayer for Christian reunion within the One, Holy, Catholic and Apostolic Church.

Nimble horses carried the Sisters up tortuous cork-screw mountain paths to Sagada in northern Luzon, where they lived in a simple hut and nursed and taught among the head-hunting Igorots. Gentle in many ways, the Igorots believed that the beheading of an enemy was evidence of superior nobility and courage. When the Sisters' handy-man reverted to this pagan practice,

and went into hiding, they were beseiged with visitors offering to betroth their children to his children. With this same alacrity, the Filipino sought schooling. The Sisters had the satisfaction of seeing little brown boys in g-strings grow up to become government officials, teachers, priests and a Bishop. Filipina women founded their own religious community.

CHAPTER THIRTEEN

Direction

T HE DEPARTURES of Father McGarvey and Mother
Edith left the Community in what first appeared to be
a state of perpetual disorganization. Mother Edith had
been both Mother Provincial of the Eastern Province and
Mother General of the entire Community. No step could be
taken to fill her offices and provide legal executors until a
Chaplain General was elected, for Father J. O. S. Huntington,
the Chaplain Provincial, was powerless under the Constitutions to effect the re-organization. A further difficulty was
that all the Bishops were in England attending the Lambeth
Conference, including the Community's Episcopal Visitors,
whose consent was necessary for the election of a Chaplain
General.

With everything stopped at dead center, it was evident
that some Sister must assume responsibility for arranging
the elections and obtaining the consents. Sister Virginia stepped into the gap, assuming the role of Assistant Mother

General, though no such officer was provided in the Constitutions. In consultation with Sister Catharine, the senior Sister in rank of profession, Sister Virginia began the tedious task of reconstruction.

Fortunately, during the June before her departure, Mother Edith had written to members of the General Council, asking their consent to call a meeting of the General Chapter and to nominate the Rev. Shirley Carter Hughson, O.H.C., as Chaplain General. Had Mother Edith not taken this step, it is doubtful if even Strong and Cadwalader*, the Community's legal advisers, could have found a way to restore its corporate life.

Father Hughson had served most acceptably as Chaplain of the Southern Province, and consent was duly given, but the Sisters thought it expedient to find out whether or not he would accept the office before summoning a General Chapter. To their inquiry he replied that his professional ethics prevented his accepting an office to which he had not been elected. Time was precious, so two Sisters were dispatched to Holy Cross Monastery at West Park, across the Hudson River. Their efforts were rewarded when Father Hughson pledged his acceptance if elected.

Accordingly, the General Chapter convened on August 1, 1908, with Mother Margaret Clare of the Western Province presiding. After Father Hughson's election, the following letter was read:

In response to the request made me, I do formally notify you that on the sixth day of July, 1908, I ceased to act as Mother

---

*The firm became Cadwalader, Wickersham and Taft in 1914.

Superior General, C.S.M., and that the office then became *ipso factor* vacant.

Respectfully, A. Edith Pardee

The Chapter then voted unanimously to separate the offices of Mother General and Mother Provincial. Adjourning to St. Mary's Chapel, the Chapter elected Sister Catharine as Mother General. A subsequent Chapter of the Eastern Province elected Sister Virginia as Mother Provincial, and on September 2 all three new officers were formally installed by Bishop William Walter Webb, just returned from Lambeth. It was a day of relief and rejoicing, yet of apprehension. "My only thought," wrote Father Hughson six years later,

> was to go straight forward, but walking softly all the days of our life, prepared to see old friends fall away, and men everywhere suspect, if not despise, us; with perhaps little or nothing in the way of the blessing of growth since souls would shrink from trusting themselves to us. . .

Father Hughson succeeded Father Huntington as Chaplain Provincial in 1911 and was in a position to see how different from his dire prediction was the decade 1908-1918. The period was marked by many professions, a deepened devotion, the building of new Convents in Kenosha and Sewanee, new school buildings at Sewanee and Peekskill, the opening of a missionary work in the Philippine Islands and the adoption of the Benedictine breviary.

Canon Winfred Douglas made the English translation of the breviary from the Breviarium Monasticum. This was essentially the same book which came to England with St. Augustine, first Archbishop of Canterbury; it was the prayer book of the Venerable Bede, St. Dunstan and St. Anselm. In urging the adoption of this book, Mother Catharine pointed out,

> we are but claiming our own heritage as members of the Anglican Church. For during one thousand years no other Book of Hours was in more general use throughout the length and breadth of England.

She appealed to the Sisters' pride and "laudable ambition" by pointing out the honor of publishing the Benedictine breviary:

> That any American Community should be the first to give back to the Church one of her most ancient office books in the words of our own mother tongue and adapted to our own Book of Common Prayer, and should furthermore be able to render the offices in all the beauty and dignity of their ancient historic setting, seems a most significant and worthy step forward.

She advised the Sisters to disregard any notion of bowdlerizing the book, insisting that their foremost aim must be to avoid all eclecticism. She instructed members of the General Chapter:

> Have clearly in mind that the proposition is not whether we shall take one part of the Benedictine Breviary and reject another, but whether we shall accept it as it stands.

On July 10, 1912, the General Chapter voted to authorize the publication of the Monastic Breviary for use in the Community. It was to be 1918, however, before the publication could be accomplished. The Order of Matins was published in 1916.

Mother Catharine can be credited with demanding of the Sisters the strict observance which she thought was clearly

178

specified in the Rule. In 1914 she issued an historic directive on religious enclosure, quoting the Rule, and adding, "It is difficult to understand how the English language could be more definite." She concluded the directive with the sage observation:

> No religious community ever became extinct from having observed too strictly the spirit of enclosure or from having spent too much time in prayer.

As the Community's reputation grew, it was asked to aid younger communities in England and Australia in formulating or reformulating their rules or in adoption of plainsong settings for the Divine Office. For example, in 1910 Mother Catharine was asked to advise the Rev. William F. Penruddocke in the revision of a rule for the Community of St. Wilfrid in Exeter.

As the Community approached the half-century mark, the Sisters began to be conscious of their place in history. Mother Catharine asked Superiors to supply data for a projected history of the Community. That volume was, in fact, never written, but the material gathered at that time made the present work possible.

The total achievement of Mother Virginia and the Reverend Mother Catharine in giving the Community new goals and strengthening it to achieve them, after the debacle of 1908, cannot be too highly praised. Their contribution, Mother Margaret Clare declared, constituted a greater work than founding a new Community. "Integrity and simplicity have done wonders," she wrote.

Simplicity and integrity finally won out in the abolition of the Order of Minor Sisters, ten of whom came into Choir amid great rejoicing on February 2, 1915. Many of the distinctions between Minor Sisters and Choir Sisters had already been abolished. They were originally under the direction of a Mistress of Minors who directed their reading and meditations, supervised their library and presided at their recreation. In early days, they were not required to contribute the $250 then required each year of Choir Sisters able to pay it, and the Choir Novices ranked ahead of professed Minors. In 1906, the Community seemed ready to abolish all distinctions, but mostly through the efforts of Mother Edith, the Order itself was retained for a decade. Changes in the Rule reduced the gulf, however; the Minors' Mistress vanished and they came under the direction of the Mother Superior. Their separate recreation and blue habit went and their years of training were reduced from four to three. They still attended only four Offices daily, and still had no share in Community government. The decision as to whether a Novice should be a Choir or Minor Sister was made by the Mother and the Mistress of Novices before a Postulant received the habit, depending upon her abilities and education. In all, only seventeen Sisters ever ranked as Minors, several having begged for assignment to that rank as an act of humility. One was a trained teacher and another the daughter of a distinguished New York family. The last of the Minor Sisters, Sister Lois, died in 1958, closing an era that few would bring back if they could.

II

If the abolition of the Minors provided an interesting footnote to history, so indeed did the Community's first venture into the foreign mission field. The idea was advanced by a

Sister after a long retreat, and tentative inquiries made to the Rt. Rev. Charles Henry Brent, Missionary Bishop of the Philippine Islands. On June 9, 1916, Bishop Brent and the Rev. John A. Staunton of Sagada, P.I., visited Peekskill and described the work for the Sisters. On January 16, 1917, three Sisters started for Sagada with Sister Mary Sylvia as their Superior.

From their discovery by Magellan in 1521 to their seizure by the United States in 1898, the Philippines had been under the rule of His Most Catholic Majesty the King of Spain. Ninety per cent of the population was Christian by the outbreak of World War I. It was with no design of "Christianizing" the Filipino, as President McKinley somewhat naively termed it, that the Rt. Rev. Charles Henry Brent had sailed for Manila in 1902, on the same ship which carried the new Governor General, William Howard Taft. Bishop Brent's intention was to minister to the American officials and army personnel, and to help establish a system of public schools. Only after he had made an extended trip through northern Luzon with the acting inspector of schools, Father John A. Staunton, Jr., did Bishop Brent realize that the head-hunting Igorots lived in mountains so rugged that Roman Catholic missionaries had never penetrated them.

In 1904 Bishop Brent sent Father Staunton to find a suitable place for establishing a mission station. A week's hard journey over perilous trails brought him to a point near Sagada, five thousand feet above sea level. He was welcomed by Senor Jaime Masferre, a former officer in the Spanish army who had married a Filipina and settled on a coffee plantation. Father Staunton and his wife, a trained nurse, lived in a goat shed for eight months, dispensing medicine and offering Mass in the doorway where the curious could watch from a safe distance. More than a hundred of the onlookers became inquirers during those first months, and eventually were baptized.

Before his ordination, Father Staunton had been an engineer. He saw at once the natural resources waiting to be utilized if only they could procure the tools—magnificent timber and a nearby waterfall, but no sawmill; stone waiting to be quarried, and so on. Undaunted, he set about to obtain the necessary machinery. Every part had to be shipped from the United States, brought by steamer up the coast and carried overland on men's shoulders a four-day journey over two mountain ranges, with several ascents and descents of some five thousand feet. Four years of unremitting work, constant delay and disappointment followed. Sometimes there were no *cargadores* (carriers) because everyone was in the rice paddies or there was no money to pay them. Sometimes a typhoon lashed the coastal steamer up and down the coast for days while precious work already done was washing down the mountain. In spite of all, four quarries were opened and a lime kiln set up. At last the sawmill was in operation and cutting the best lumber outside Manila.

In directing the Mission's many enterprises, Father Staunton was scrupulously just and humane. The workers learned that what he promised he paid, fairly and regularly, and that they were always treated as men, not as beasts of burden. The Igorots, whose only diversion was head-hunting among enemy tribes, began to take pride in their Mission. When excavation for a new hospital began, crowds overflowed the little wooden church. By May, 1908, the baptisms numbered over five hundred. In Lent throngs of workmen from the

182

rice terraces stopped by each Friday to say the Stations of the Cross, dressed in the customary G-string, a bit of cloth the size of a necktie.

The religion of the Igorots was animistic. They lived in terror of "anitos," the spirits of the dead, which they believed dwelt in trees and rocks and required propitiation in the form of animal sacrifice. The Stauntons organized expeditions to the haunted caves, to encourage youngsters to overcome their fears.

Mrs. Staunton taught classes in weaving, lace-making and crocheting, as well as ordinary homemaking skills. In 1912 Father Staunton began construction on the great stone church, he himself acting as architect and engineer of every operation: logging, planing, carpentering, blacksmithing, blasting, excavation, stone-cutting and masonry. The structure was built to withstand typhoon winds up to one hundred miles an hour. The buttresses were placed inside the building, forming five bays on each side of the nave. By 1921 the building was completed.

The rising walls of the great church greeted the Sisters when they arrived late in February, 1917, after a journey by horseback along narrow paths cut out of the mountain side, with drop-offs of a thousand feet a few inches from their horses' hoofs. They were welcomed to the Mission by enthusiastic schoolgirls, by the Stauntons, who had fixed up the little Mission office building for their temporary living quarters, and by Father and Mrs. Bartter, who were to be such good friends in days to come.

The temporary house was in the middle of a road along which thronged hundreds of Filipinos on their way to the fields each day. Soon the women and children were stopping in for a chat or to consult Sister Mary Sylvia, a registered nurse. She quickly set up nursing clinics at each of the three out-stations of the Mission. Sister Monica established a sewing class for the young women. Sister Mary Michael began classes among the younger children. By the time of Bishop Brent's next visitation, the Sisters were well established as part of the Mission family.

GLADYS RICE WASHBURN

Massive walls of granite matched by outcroppings on nearby slopes give to St. Mary's Chapel and Convent, Peekskill, an air of extraordinary solidity, integrity and serene strength.

Nestled in a mountain valley 7,200 feet high, St. Raphael's Retreat House at Evergreen, Colorado, shown here in 1930, was the means of introducing retreats in many western dioceses.

Associates, pledged to support the Sisters with prayer and alms, frequently contribute their skills and time, as well. Below: cataloguing books at the House of the Redeemer.

CHAPTER FOURTEEN

Flowering

THE YEAR 1918 MARKED the end of an era in the history of the Community. Sister Margaret Clare, the vigorous administrator and trail-blazer, resigned as Mother Superior of the Western Province and was succeeded by Sister Mary Maude, student and mystic and director of souls. In the Eastern Province Mother Virginia was succeeded by Sister Mary Theodora, destined to serve as Mother Superior of that Province for twenty-five years. The Mother General elected that year to succeed Mother Catharine was Sister Mary Veronica, well known in the Church as an ecclesiastical artist of great distinction but most beloved by her Sisters for her gentle concern and kindness toward the perplexed. Father Hughson resigned as Chaplain General that year and was succeeded by a parish priest, the distinguished rector of St. Mark's Church, Philadelphia, the Rev. Frank Lawrence Vernon.

Disparate as the new Superiors were in temperament, they

shared common ideals and goals. During this era, prodded by World War I and the fabric shortage, the Community had voted to discard their Victorian attire, voluminous with pleats and flowing train. They had adopted a habit of simple cut with the traditional monastic scapular, or flap-apron. The change from train to scapular symbolized the movement toward a modified Benedictine ethos which the Community's leaders desired.

The dynamo of this development was Mother Mary Theodora. From 1908, when she became Assistant Superior, until her retirement in 1943, she strove to guide the Community to a fuller expression of the Benedictine ideals of withdrawal, prayer and work. Even in old age, sick and blind, she continued to teach, exhort and advise her Sisters in the way she was sure they should go. The Superiors of the Community have been, without exception, women of high purpose. Some have been distinguished by gentle goodness, some by a towering strength of intellect and will, some few by true and selfless greatness. Sister Mary Theodora was strong. Wellesley-educated, she was one of the first Sisters with a bachelor's degree. A convert from Methodism and a daughter of the manse, her election to profession in 1905 and her subsequent service as secretary to Mother Edith gave her a close-hand view of the tragedy of 1908. Ever after, she recoiled from tendencies toward sentimental excesses and finally came to place her entire trust in Benedictine monachism.

Equally gifted and influential, though in a radically different area, was Mother Mary Maude. Superior of St. Mary's School in Memphis, then of St. Mary's School, Peekskill, she served briefly as Mother of the Western Province, then as Novice Mistress in Peekskill and as Mother General for nineteen years. A self-taught linguist, she began her study of Hebrew in her fiftieth year and attained a scholar's proficiency in that and other ancient tongues. As a woman of prayer and a spiritual director, she represented that hidden, interior life of the Community which is more profoundly effectual than its exterior polity. No one has yet measured, nor is likely to measure, the importance and influence in the world of hardships sweetly borne, of sickness and sorrow and disappointment accepted with serene faith, of failure met courageously and scornful malice quickly forgiven. These lessons, and many other lessons in true Catholic spirituality, were bequeathed to the Community by Mother Mary Maude. Whether in scholarly journals, in Novitiate classes or in letters to perplexed souls, she was primarily a woman of faith and prayer sharing her treasure. She built with something more enduring than bricks and mortar. Among the names on the Community's bede roll are many names of Sisters who struggled, failed, and finally triumphed in the hard school of holiness, the one work which endures.

Reverend Mother Mary Veronica was also tender and deft in her handling of individual Sisters. Intense and imaginative, she retained unusual vitality and resilience into old age, providing an important link between two eras. When in the sixties it was noticed that the only full-scale portrait of her in the archives was an exquisite pencil-sketch profile study of a beautiful girl in a picture hat, her Superior asked her to sit for a photograph. Though she had always resisted being photographed as inconsistent with her concept of the hidden life, she consented simply and sat for her first photograph, aged nearly ninety.

Though Sister Mary Veronica herself shrank from the

camera, she was the instrument of portraying dozens of distinguished Churchmen and statesmen. One of the splendid portraits she painted was of "Ma Garner", the matriarch of the Cumberland plateau. Most of her work was executed in a technique of the Italian Renaissance, which she developed after extensive study in Italy of the frescoes of Fra Angelico. The medium was pigment mixed with wax and mastic, frequently applied to a linen-textured surface.

Three of the Community's Chaplains figure prominently in its history from 1920 to the 1940's. Preeminent was the Rev. Shirley Carter Hughson, O.H.C., who had served so well as Chaplain General from 1908 to 1918. As Chaplain of the Eastern Province from 1911 to 1941, he spared no effort to deepen the Sisters' dedication and strengthen their resolve. The years that softened his strangely simian facial features and damped down his fiery disposition only accentuated his faith and fervor. In all the houses of the Community, Father Hughson was remembered with love and laughter for the way he descended like a windstorm, calling for a Sister to take his laundry, done up in an untidy package, and requiring a Sister-stenographer to take hours of dictation in an effort to dispose of his voluminous correspondence. His counsel was cherished by generations of Sisters, and he alone of all the Community's spiritual shepherds figures in a tale of the miraculous. An older Sister, a woman of great common sense, confided that Father Hughson appeared to her after his death, when she was facing dangerous surgery, and re-assured her in his fatherly, matter-of-fact way.

Complementing Father Hughson was his successor as Chaplain General, the Rev. Frank L. Vernon. Born in Canada, Father Vernon received the call to the priesthood when he was fourteen, after making his first confession. He wrote:

> It was the working use of Penance and Communion, stimu-
> lating a prayer life, that gave me an experiential knowledge
> of God and of grace and of the Church, of revealed truth, of
> the intercessory labor of the saints and the ministry of the
> angels. It took me over the frontier and into the outlying
> country, in the midst of which I could always sense and some-
> times see the shining City of God.

This sense and sight Father Vernon communicated to the Sisters in retreats and instructions, in strikingly original expositions of the gospel still used in Novitiate classes long years after his death. Rector of a downtown parish, Father Vernon yet maintained a disciplined devotion and constant study of ascetical and mystical theology. His mastery of the principles of the cloistered life enabled him to speak with utmost authority, and his insight into human nature and needs won over the most recalcitrant. Father Vernon's daughter entered the Community and became the beloved headmistress of St. Mary's School, Peekskill.

Less influential by reason of his limited sphere and untimely death, the Very Rev. Rowland Frederick Philbrook, Dean of Trinity Cathedral in Davenport, Iowa, and Chaplain of the Western Province for two years until 1946, nevertheless played an important role in the Community's apostolate. As friend and confessor of the Sisters at St. Katharine's School, Father Philbrook strengthened their Catholic mission in a most vital way by his firm grasp of theology and liturgy, combined with a winsome kindness and quizzical humor.

II

No account of the Community's leadership in the first

decades of the century would be adequate without tribute to the Community's choir master for nearly forty years, the distinguished pioneer of the plainsong revival, the Rev. Canon Charles Winfred Douglas. His patient teaching, exhaustive research and splendid translations bore fruit in a perfection of worship never before known in the American Church, for he represented the link with the greatest Benedictine traditions.

"Three days before John Keble preached his Assize sermon in 1833," wrote Father Douglas in his *Church Music in History and Practice,*

> a young French priest, Prosper Gueranger, left his home in Sable, Sarthe, and with a few companions, walked to the unoccupied tenth-century priory Church of St. Peter, Solesmes. There they knelt in the presence of God and dedicated themselves to the restoration of the monastic life in France, which had been deprived of it since the Revolution. The new Benedictine community founded by them devoted itself to liturgical studies, and eventually to an intensive examination of all existing remains of early Christian music.

On the Feast of the Transfiguration, 1899, Winfred Douglas knelt in the tiny Mission of the Transfiguration, Evergreen, Colorado, and offered to God his manifold talents, with all the fame and fortune they would have brought him, in exchange for priesthood in the Church. Surrender brought its hundred-fold reward in a manner no human intelligence could have predicted.

In 1903 Father Douglas travelled to the Isle of Wight, to study with the Benedictine monks exiled there from their monastery at Solesmes. Here, with other priests and choir masters, he absorbed the instructions of Dom Mocquereau and Dom Eudine, and soared to the gate of heaven on the chanting of the Offices and Mass.

But how was he to put his new knowledge to practical use? Parish churches in America were subject to changing policy with changing rectorships. It occurred to Father Douglas that a school or seminary might offer a more fixed policy within which he could work. Above all, a religious community appealed to him, especially the Community of Saint Mary, by reason of its increasing development of the contemplative life and its provision for recitation of the Divine Office in Choir. He was delighted when, soon after his return to New York in 1906, he received an invitation from Mother Margaret Clare to visit Kenosha and instruct the Sisters in the chant. She had heard plainsong at the Convent of Saint Mary the Virgin in Wantage, England, and, with that decisiveness that marked her every move, had determined that the Community must adopt the Solesmes style of chanting.

The Superiors at Peekskill followed suit. In December, 1906, Father Douglas became choir master on Mount Saint Gabriel and immediately began to provide a musical setting of the Community Ceremonial. He found that the Sisters had been using a form of psalmody called "murmuring," with adaptations of modern music for other portions of the liturgy. Within ten days Father Douglas had them singing Compline to authentic plainsong modes, and within a few weeks the other offices were undertaken with gratifying success. To put it thus, of course, is to oversimplify an arduous undertaking. Some hint of what was involved is implied in an article Canon Douglas prepared for the March, 1926, issue of *The Catholic Choirmaster:*

Our work began with exhaustive study of psalmody on the

193

part of the Sisters, week after week analyzing and practicing the simpler mediations and endings until all could sing them naturally from the unpointed text, and the organist could unfailingly give the necessary support at points of rhythmic impulse. Old habits of hard, unvarying rhythm had to be eradicated, a task of long patience. Then, little by little, the melodies of the more important Office Hymns were undertaken and mastered in their true rhythms.

Father Douglas next turned to teaching the music of the Mass to the girls of St. Mary's School. They soon let him know their views on this strange music:

> . . . they were loud in their objections. Beauty and interest were to be banished. Nobody was to sing alto any more; solos were to disappear; there was neither time nor tune to this dreadful Plain-song! Many a tear was shed over the hard necessity of everybody rehearsing such unattractive music. However, we persevered; and within a year had a fairly creditable singing of *Missa de Angelis,* chosen as being least likely to offend minds accustomed only to the major scale.

In 1910 Father Douglas brought his family to Mount Saint Gabriel. Here, near the entrance to the grounds, they occupied for twelve years a stone house which he named St. Dunstan's in honor of the great Archbishop of Canterbury who was a skilled musician. Here he began adapting the antiphons of the Divine Office from the Benedictine manuscripts known as the Hartker Antiphoner, the Worcester Antiphoner and the Lucca Antiphoner, as well as from Solesmes and Vatican sources. Of the variant forms, he chose the one best suited to the English adaptation. He then wrote out the first antiphons in his own hand to be copied by the Sisters. After trying them, he would make changes, not once but several times, and the Sisters would be obliged to re-copy their copies. Mimeographed sheets were next, and finally the printed editions of Psalter, Canticles, Ceremonial and Masses. In addition to the series of musical publications, the translation of the Benedictine Breviary was undertaken under Canon Douglas' direction. The first edition of the Night Offices was privately printed in 1916 and of the Day Offices in 1918. By 1926 Father Douglas could write:

> It was just twenty years after the Sisters' first lesson in psalmody that they sang a vespers complete in every musical detail.

Throughout this long process, Father Douglas exhibited his own rare combination of patience, enthusiasm, humor and outgoing sympathy. Rehearsing the Sisters in a difficult setting of the profession office, he would seat himself at the piano with the announcement, "I'll be the Novice." He entered into all the life of the hilltop, preaching, conducting retreats, hearing confessions, and joining in the school festivities. He organized the Christmas Pageant at St. Mary's School, to this day a favorite feature of the school year. Generations of schoolgirls remembered him in his own special role of Good King Wenceslas, played with utmost devotion. An alumna wrote:

> My earliest recollections of St. Mary's are the Sunday evenings when he played Bach for us on the piano in the reception room off the Stone Corridor, and brought to us the realization that Bach's music was full of deep emotion and spiritual fineness, as well as of the technical difficulties which caused us such travail. . . Among my most treasured memories are the recollections of Sunday dinners at St. Dunstan's with Mrs. Douglas and Father Douglas, followed by delightful afternoons of music with Father Douglas at the organ in his music room, while some of us students had the honor of playing the violin or the piano or singing with his organ accompaniment.

Everything Father Douglas touched had a way of becoming merry and joyful—even committee meetings. DeKoven Foundation in Racine was the scene of the final meetings of the revision committee preparing the Hymnal 1940 for presentation to the General Convention. Aware of the historic significance of the meetings, the Sisters were amused more than once to hear whoops of laughter from within the conference room. Many years before, upon checking over the *Ceremonial Noted,* Dom Eudine had exclaimed, "Ah! Pere Doo-glass, you have robbed us well!" That robbery now enriched the entire American Church.

Father Douglas died on January 18, 1944, in Santa Rosa, California, having composed a piece for organ earlier in the day. He had finished every work but one—the Antiphoner was still in manuscript at the time of his death. Sister Hildegarde, Assistant Superior of the Western Province and a skilled musician, assisted by Sister Benedicta, attended to the final revision and publication in 1954 of *The Diurnal Noted,* as it was titled. It was quickly adopted by some twenty communities in America, England, Australia, Tasmania, Africa and South America.

The Community magazine, *St. Mary's Messenger,* cited as his monumental work the translation into English of the Benedictine Breviary and the provision of authentic musical settings:

> Since the middle of the sixth century down to the present time there has never been a day, scarcely an hour, when somewhere in the world the divine praises were not being sung in the Latin text of the Monastic Office. Now through the work of Father Douglas the same praises ascend in our own mother tongue.

196

III

Distinguished leadership coupled with steady devotion to allay suspicion and restore the Community to a place of trust and confidence. In demonstration of this fact, Mother Harriet was honored during the twenties by several memorials depicting the establishment of the religious life in the American Episcopal Church. Even before the Great War, St. John's Church, Newport, Rhode Island, included her in an altar painting in the Lady Chapel, completed in 1914. After the War, St. Luke's Chapel in New York installed a small statue of her in the Chapel of the Blessed Sacrament, the one-time sacristy where she had first been elected Superior. A statue was installed in the Lady Chapel of the Church of the Advent, Boston, a stained glass window in St. Clement's Church, Philadelphia, and windows were placed in the Bishops' House at the Cathedral of SS. Peter and Paul in Washington and in the Church of the Atonement, Chicago. A descriptive pamphlet issued by the Church of the Holy Cross, Kingston, New York, in alluding to a statue of Mother Harriet in the reredos, described it as "in the lowest niche on the left," a placement she herself would have regarded as most suitable.

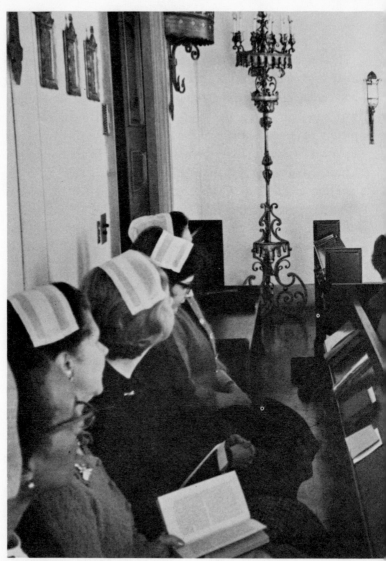

Retreatants at the House of the Redeemer, New York, listening to a retreat

GLADYS RICE WASHBURN

address delivered by the Rev. Paul C. Weed, Jr., vicar of St. Luke's Chapel.

CHAPTER FIFTEEN

Sagada

HOSTILITY FAILED TO DISLODGE the Community from its western outpost in Davenport, but the combination of poverty, the Great Depression and finally World War II compelled the Sisters to withdraw from St. Katharine's in 1943, not without great sorrow. No work of the Community ever inspired greater affection, on the part of the Sisters, alumnae and staff. The Sisters liked to think that those forty years in Davenport had helped to nurture the Church in the area to vigor, breadth and zeal. This indeed had been suggested earlier in a letter to Peekskill by the Rt. Rev. Theodore N. Morrison:

> If you knew the condition of Church life in Iowa in days gone by—the hostility to Catholic teaching and practices—and then could appreciate what the Sisters have done to bring about among the people a broader, more intelligent and more sympathetic attitude toward the Church's teaching and worship, you would feel, I am sure, as I do, that the work has been

blessed of God and the results are not to be measured by statistics giving the number of girls enrolled or by the balance sheet of the treasurer.

The removal of the Community from a time-honored and beloved work is always a time of testing. The Community's continued existence depends at such times on the Sisters who give to obedience the priority it clearly requires. What such changes cost could be guessed by acquaintance with any of the Sisters withdrawn from the mission houses in New York and Chicago when those two works were relinquished. With loyalty, humility and costing obedience, they purchased peace and continuing life for their Community.

The strength and flexibility required for change from one work to another was also demanded in cases where a radical departure from former goals created an entirely new work within the framework of an older institution. A sweeping change came to the Sewanee community in the forties, when construction of the Dixie Highway and other roads made it possible for school buses to transport the children of the Cumberland Plateau to the schools which the Works Progress Administration had built during the Depression. A mission boarding school was no longer required. A college preparatory school for daughters of the faculty at the University of the South was needed, and the Vice Chancellor of the University persuaded the Sisters that such a program was feasible. St. Mary's-on-the-Mountain quickly won a following and within ten years had been fully accredited by the Southern Association for Secondary Schools and Colleges. By 1965 a splendid new dormitory crowned the bluff, beside a new building housing classrooms, library and laboratories. Expanded facilities made it possible for the Sisters to extend the important program of retreats for Associates and friends.

St. Mary's Hospital in New York adapted its services to the growing need for a children's convalescent hospital. A bequest from the estate of lumberman Henry S. K. Williams made possible the purchase of a six-acre site overlooking Belt Parkway and Little Neck Bay in Bayside, Long Island, where the Community erected a million-dollar hospital of one hundred beds. Subsequent gifts made possible an extensive department of rehabilitation medicine, opened in 1960. Physical therapy, occupational therapy and speech therapy were thereby provided for children four to twelve suffering from neuromuscular disability, bone and joint malformation or disease, sequelae of trauma, burns and infections, including poliomyelitis and encephalitis, vegetative dysfunctions and bronchial asthma. Post-operative rehabilitation for lung and heart surgery cases was also provided. The new program was integrated with the Training School for Infant and Child Care, which gives its students basic skills in pediatric rehabilitation.

The last decades of the century saw a series of changes in the Community's oldest work, the House of Mercy. When in 1920 the property at 214th Street and Bolton Road in northern Manhattan was condemned to make a public park, the work was moved to a farm near Valhalla in eastern Westchester County. Here on a gently sloping hill was built St. Mary's-in-the-Field, with gardens, orchards and tree-lined lanes. At the same time the trustees transferred the trusteeship to the Sisters, and in 1924 the charter was amended to define the purpose as centering on the care of abandoned, delinquent or neglected children over twelve.

In its long span of development from the dreary days of

201

Dickens to present-day methods, the work achieved notable success, but not without mismoves. One of these attracted much unfavorable notice. In 1920, after sixty-six years of accepting all races, the Sisters began to refuse admission to Negro girls. Superiors indicated that racial differences presented insurmountable difficulties when they were added to the multiple problems of treating disturbed and delinquent girls. In 1942 this policy gave rise to a storm of unfavorable publicity and sharp criticism by public welfare officers. The New York City Welfare Department threatened to withdraw its dependents from five Protestant institutions unless they complied with a non-segregation statute. Two secondary factors influenced the Sisters' decision to withstand this order: the city's action was taken precipitately, with more regard to its political uses than to the welfare of the children involved; and the threats sounded a trifle bombastic in view of the fact that city funds at that time provided only about half the cost of maintaining each child with minimum custodial care. Mother Mary Theodora denied that race prejudice was behind the policy, and the issue was debated throughout the summer, with welfare officials growing more coldly critical and the Mother increasingly adamant. On October 19, New York Mayor Fiorello LaGuardia, himself a loyal Churchman, pleaded with the Sisters to reconsider their decision, adding kindly, "Your Board and your staff occupy a position of dignity and distinction in the field of child care."

The story broke in the morning editions of October 30, with the *New York Times* and other papers naming the five offending institutions and pointing out that twenty-four Roman Catholic and five Jewish institutions had bowed to the non-segregation statute. The Community's legal representatives begged the Superior for permission to issue a statement in defense; she authorized a brief statement, but one hardly calculated to court public favor. In a letter to the Superior at St. Mary's-in-the-Field, the Mother insisted stoutly, "We shall just have to grin and bear it." Whatever the justice or wisdom of the Community's stand in 1942, it was widely misinterpreted and was later reversed.

A sweeping change took place quietly at St. Mary's Home in Chicago in the forties when institutional care gave way to foster home care. Studies by trained social welfare workers prompted the Sisters to sell the building on West Jackson Blvd. and buy property at 5741 North Kenmore suitable to the needs of a foster home and adoption agency. Between seventy and eighty children, from the newly born to teen agers, could be cared for in this way. Behind each child was a tragic story of illness, mental or physical; of destitution, drunkenness or drug-addiction; of cruelty, desertion or parental moral unfitness. Every effort is made to reunite parents and children, but when this is impossible, the child is placed in an adoptive home or a foster home. In some cases this is possible only after extensive medical and psychiatric treatment. The Sisters and a staff of trained case workers see that each child receives what he needs by way of home care, medical and dental care, school expenses and clothing. The generosity of friends enables the Sisters to meet an annual budget in excess of $90,000 and late in 1964 plans were made to erect a remedial treatment center for the emotionally disturbed.

II

World War II found three Sisters of Saint Mary interned

in a Japanese prison camp in northern Luzon. For them, for the other members of the Mission staff at Sagada, and for the Igorot Christians, the War was an ultimate test of devotion and loyalty. The quiet heroism and true Christian community displayed during the Japanese occupation of the Philippines, the patient endurance of the prisoners and the self-sacrificing generosity of the Christians from Sagada and Bontoc, were tribute enough, if tribute was needed, to the sound teaching of Father Staunton.

As early as 1916, the very vision and ingenuity which characterized Father Staunton's work in Luzon had made him impatient of officialdom and had earned the disfavor of the Board of Missions. Bishop Brent defended him that year before the Board, citing his extraordinary gifts:

> He has been misunderstood, at times even by myself. It is only comparatively recently that I have given the man his full measure. The mission that he represents is not a station, it is a diocese. He is the chief spiritual influence in the entire country; he is the best-informed man, whether in government or in business . . . his advice is sought by officials who represent the American government; he is on friendly terms with the Roman Church clergy who are laboring in that district. . . There were times when I thought I could teach Father Staunton better ways of doing his work than those he has learned from God Himself. I have ceased to interject my own theories into the life of a man who has proved by his work that he knows how to bring simple-minded people into close and intimate touch with God as revealed in Jesus Christ.

Bishop Brent's resignation was the beginning of dissension that broke Father Staunton. A new bishop did not take over until 1920, and in the two-year interval Bishop Graves of Shanghai was in charge. On his visitation to Sagada he appeared to be pleased with its progress, but shortly afterward he issued an encyclical to the clergy of the missionary district, condemning:

> First, the practice of "Reservation of the Blessed Sacrament" (except for Communion of the Sick) and the burning of a light before it.
> Second, the singing of the Ave Maria together with the burning of candles and offering of flowers before the image of the Virgin.

However well-intentioned these strictures were, their effect on the Mission staff and the people of Sagada was devastating. Father Staunton replied in an open letter which he sent to Bishops and others in authority, pointing out that Bishop Brent had permitted the devotions which Bishop Graves condemned, and that similar practices might be found in a hundred or more parishes in the United States.

The election of the Rt. Rev. Gouverneur Frank Mosher brought hope of help instead of condemnation from missionary district authorities. Father Staunton wrote enthusiastically that Bishop Mosher was working out a plan of using native catechists who, it was hoped, would provide native candidates for the ministry. Father Staunton added:

> We are evidently, under Bishop Mosher's leadership, on the verge of great things to the glory of our Church and the blessing of these mountain people.

But criticism of Father Staunton continued, in the form of directives issued from New York. Father Staunton's health declined, and he suffered a sunstroke from which he never fully recovered. In his discouragement and anxiety, he and four other priests in the Mountain Province submitted resignations. It is doubtful that they anticipated acceptance, but

Bishop Mosher replied immediately, accepting the resignations, and so Father Staunton's connection with the Mission
ended. He asked the officials in New York for an opportunity
to state his case, but his plea was met by silence. Heart-
broken, he returned to the United States, made his submission
to the Roman Catholic Church, and obtained a position at
the University of Notre Dame, where his brother was a professor. After Mrs. Staunton's death he went to Rome to study
for ordination and, though suffering from glaucoma, was
ordained. Sadly, failing eyesight soon made it impossible for
him to exercise his priesthood.

The Sisters and other Mission staff stayed on, though the
personnel of the Sisters' house changed from time to time. In
March, 1929, Sisters Felicitas and Brigit died of poisoning
when a native girl accidentally used rat poison in baking. The
Community withdrew temporarily from the work, but resumed it in the early thirties.

The deaths of the two Sisters, and the sufferings and dere-
liction of Father Staunton, who died thinking his work at
Sagada a failure, as well as the labors and trials of all the
Mission staff who persevered in spite of official disfavor, all
were to bear fruit when the war brought the Islands under
a Japanese military dictatorship. In December, 1940, two
Filipino women were professed in a native order, the Sisters
of Saint Mary the Virgin, which undertook the direction of
an orphanage. On June 4, 1941, Eduardo Longid was ordained to the priesthood, and two days later Albert Masferre
was ordained in Bontoc.*

*In 1962 Father Longid was consecrated Bishop and became suffra-
gan under the Rt. Rev. Lyman Ogilby; Father Masferre died in
1963.

In the midst of the Fiesta of the Conception of Our Lady, December 8, 1941, came the news of Pearl Harbor, to which the reports added that Camp John Hay had been bombed. Not long after, invading Japanese troops brought in bundles of pesos they had printed in preparation for the invasion, and prices immediately sky-rocketed. The Igorots built huts and gardens high in the mountains, but it was soon apparent that much suffering lay ahead for them. When General Douglas MacArthur offered missionaries transportation to safety, the Mission staff at Sagada decided to remain. Then missionary personnel were commanded by the Japanese to appear in Bontoc no later than 5 p.m. on May 25, 1942, or the Rev. Clifford E. B. Nobes would be shot. At 4 a.m. on May 24, the Sagada staff offered Mass and prepared to leave, bidding sad good-byes to many friends congregated to see them off. Though they had no money to hire *cargadores,* more than 150 Filipinos volunteered to carry their provisions down the tortuous corkscrew trail, the first of many acts of loving kindness which Filipinos were to perform in the terrible days ahead. After a brief stay at Bontoc, on June 16 they were ordered to Camp Holmes near Baguio. They loaded their array of washbasins, pails, pitchers, suitcases, cots and canned goods onto four trucks, which hurtled them down the hairpin curves at break-neck speed, leaving them all covered with thick coats of dust. En route they glimpsed United States military personnel, a sight that haunted them in the three years of imprisonment—gaunt, hopeless-looking prisoners of war, one of whom when he attempted to call to them, was slapped violently by a guard.

They were warmly welcomed to Camp Holmes, despite already crowded facilities. In all, six hundred internees shared the Camp's two dormitories, one for men and one for women, and the mess hall, where at first the Sisters were given a corner for sleeping. Many of the internees were missionaries representing various Christian groups, while some were mining-company executives and miners. The specialists all gave their services free for the benefit of the entire Camp—priests, doctors, dentists, nurses, electrical engineers, plumbers, carpenters and cooks. Three little tin huts, each one sixteen feet square, became "nunnery row," with the Sisters of Saint Mary sharing one hut with two lady missionaries; three Sisters of Saint Anne in another; and seven Roman Catholic Sisters of Maryknoll in the third.

Despite the irritations and frustrations of camp life, there prevailed a cheerful ingenuity among the internees. When the Sisters' door kept blowing open in typhoon winds, it was bolted for them by the distinguished architect J. Van Wie Bergamini, who was to rebuild the destroyed churches in the Philippines after the war. When cow's milk was no longer available for the camp's babies, the doctors worked hard at developing coconut and soybean milk, while the camp's erstwhile farmers imported goats and started a small dairy. When misunderstandings arose between the internees and their jailers, Miss Nellie McKim, an alumna of Kemper Hall, acted as emissary to smooth out difficulties, using her fluent Japanese and her position of trust and influence which the soldiers freely accorded her. From June, 1942, until the autumn of 1943, the camp was under Japanese civil authorities, in charge of a Mr. Tomebe who had studied at the University of California, and was humane and just. In that early period, time passed quickly, even happily. Sister Juliana taught fifth grade in the camp school, which enrolled about one hundred children. Sister Columba and Sister Mary Oliva worked on a kitchen crew headed by a Seventh Day Adventist missionary, extracting worms, weevils, and rubbish from the daily rice ration for the camp. They were allowed to augment the camp diet with food from the camp store and with gifts from friends outside. Bishop Wilner, Father Longid and the Filipino Sisters sent them money as they were able. The prevailing spirit of good-humored cheerfulness despite boredom, lack of news from home and inadequate diet was a perpetual puzzle to the Japanese guards.

Toward the autumn of 1943, the camp was removed from civil control and placed under the military. The new commandant, Lieutenant Cura, was so heartily detested by his own soldiers that they vowed to kill him, and his fellow officers refused to eat with him. He decreed irrational regulations and, as the Allied forces pushed the Japanese harder, near-starvation rations. A double fence was erected, and two internees escaped. The effect of this was an edict forbidding food bags to be brought in, so that only peanuts and sugar were available in the camp store. The daily rice ration gave way to coarsely ground fodder corn, with resultant illness. The chickens and vegetables the internees were able to raise were saved for "children and specials"—two chickens mixed with rice serving about one hundred of those needing better food. The commandant ordered internees aged six to fifty to work in the garden, and many kept small gardens of their own. One of the Sisters proudly produced from her garden an ear of sweet corn and four string beans, which provided a good laugh if not much nutriment. It is a tribute to human fortitude that the internees never forgot how to laugh. They even laughed at a pompous little martinet named Yamato

who strutted about at daily roll call as if he were at Bucking-
ham Palace, followed on several occasions by a soldier's pet
gander, waddling behind in striking similitude. Their growing shabbiness afforded some amusement, for the Sisters'
shoes were half-soled with slices of automobile tire which
fringed out white along the sides, giving them a dashing
"white-walled" appearance.

There were other sources of strength as well. Every day
they were privileged to offer the Holy Sacrifice of the Mass,
even if the shortage of wheat bread made it impossible to
receive Holy Communion often. On their respective patronal
festivals, the Sisters would invite the celebrating group to a
party, even if the treats consisted of cornmeal cakes, peanut
butter and hot water for beverage, as they did at the Epiphany
party of 1945. On one Feast of the Purification the Maryknoll Sisters presented the Sisters of Saint Mary with a luxurious plate of candy made over their charcoal stove. On
another candle-less Candlemas, the Sisters of Saint Anne
produced a carefully hoarded can of salmon and one of sweet
corn for a banquet which concluded with rice pudding surmounted with grape jelly. Mother Ursula, O.S.A., composed
witty commemorative poems for these occasions, in one of
which she outpunned everyone with an allusion to "our
common fete."

But perhaps the Sisters were most deeply touched and
strengthened by the devotion of the Christian communities
at Bontoc and Sagada. The people sent them millet, camotes
(sweet potatoes), rice, calcium tablets and coffee, when they
themselves were often in want. Sister Teresa, C.S.M.V., sent
them some liver early in March, the first such luxury they had
had since Christmas. Father Longid, the Filipino Sisters, and

many laymen reached out hands of love the Sisters would always recall with tears of gratitude. On one occasion, a fourteen-year-old schoolgirl, unable to gain admission to the compound, sent them money with this note:

> Dear Sisters: This is the only thing I can do to help you because yesterday I tried to buy bananas and some tomatoes but I could not bring it to you. I bought with $2.10 bananas but sorey I can't bring it to you. Hope there will be a time for me again because that is the only money I have. I sent it to Mr. Claunch when we went to pitch water. I will try to bring you again when my brother will come to get me. Hope God will ever permit you to come out in the concentration camp. God bless you forever. Just me, Rosario Colus

On the Feast of St. Mary Magdalene during a typhoon, they recited the antiphon "Many waters cannot quench love, neither can the floods drown it" as the rain poured in and splashed on their heads, drenching the Sisters and their breviaries.

Before his departure, Mr. Tomebe had arranged for Red Cross boxes to be delivered. Their arrival at Christmas in 1943 came at a time when everyone's spirits were sagging and many were in real want. Each box weighed over fifty pounds, containing cans of butter, cheese, powdered milk, chocolate, canned goods and toilet soap. There were new shoes and shirts. But when the Red Cross supplies ran out, malnutrition set in with a vengeance. The price of eggs soared to sixty cents apiece. One meal in September consisted of blood pudding from the blood of their last cow, and it became common to see people picking through the garbage for something edible. When Sister Augusta, O.S.A., told her class of little children the story of Br'er Rabbit, their only comment was, "Wouldn't they taste good?!"

The first sight of American planes, in December, 1944, filled the internees with joy, but there was worse imprisonment ahead. The Japanese ordered the evacuation of Camp Holmes. The Sisters were in one of the first departure groups, on December 28, and for the next few weeks they shared and witnessed some of the agony of "Bilibid."

The journey down to Manila was miserable, with thirty-six persons plus baggage packed into each truck and no food provided for thirty-three hours. The sight of Baguio cheered them, until the horrified expressions of the Filipinos told them what their own physical appearance must be.

The Japanese assured them that Manila had been declared an open city and that they would be given comfortable quarters there. Neither statement was true. The quarters turned out to be the old Bilibid prison, abandoned by the Japanese for a new prison. The old one was a scarred hulk of a dungeon without windows or plumbing, both of which had been removed to the new building. The mattresses they were given were so filthy and infested that they preferred to sleep on the cement floors. For more than a month the food ration was barely enough to sustain life—bean curd residue, a cup of corn meal mush with weevils much in evidence, and camote greens decayed to slime. The water was unfit for drinking, and there was no firewood to boil it.

As the Sisters knelt on a narrow parapet overlooking the courtyard, they could see below fifty rude graves where lay American service men who had died of Japanese neglect and torture. One Sister was seriously ill, and in their weakness it seemed to them they would soon lie in that courtyard cemetery. Again their lives were saved by the selfless concern of many, including a Japanese guard who smuggled in food at the risk of his own life. The gallant Father Nobes, who arrived in a later departure group from Camp Holmes, brought them money he obtained by shrewdly selling their beds to Japanese soldiers. With this money they bought six coconuts and ten ounces of peanuts, the only food available.

The Sisters noted that their mental processes declined as their physical condition worsened, and that they were unable to remember simple facts they had known all their lives. They found that drinking a little boiled water in the middle of the day lessened the pains of starvation, and at the end of the day, if their rations had been hopelessly inadequate, Sister Columba would decide whether they should each have a tiny bit of chocolate from the piece they had hoarded.

Their spirits continued to be sustained by the offering of the Holy Sacrifice. In the courtyard was a path with five caged cells on either side, said to have been torture cells. The wall of one was inscribed in pencil:

> We, the undersigned, broken in body and spirit from starvation and torture, expect those who come after us to work our vengeance on our enemies.

Below were the signatures of eight Americans. The Sisters complied in their own way—every morning they knelt in one of the cells and offered up Our Lord's redemptive life and death in union with the sufferings of the men who had formerly lived there, on behalf of the entire sinful world.

It soon became evident that Manila was by no means an open city. They were kept sleepless night after night by the shelling and the blasts of Japanese demolition. On February 2 before midnight they heard rapid gunfire from the direction

213

of the waterfront and saw seven United States planes circling. The next morning they heard Mass over the din of gunfire, and sang the Te Deum. Mr. Eschbach called them together that morning and announced that they were released. They saluted an American flag one of the internees had made, and sang "God Bless America" and "The Star-Spangled Banner." Sister Columba noted all this in her diary with the laconic comment, "I never felt more patriotic in my life."

On February 5 the old prison was threatened by the encroaching fire destroying the city. The internees, with eight hundred military prisoners, all veterans of Corregidor and Bataan who had been starved to skeletons, were moved to an abandoned shoe factory three miles outside the city. Here they were received by American military personnel, who were taking over bit by bit. They were treated with great kindness, and the Sisters, suffering from the lassitude of starvation, remembered most gratefully a Roman Catholic chaplain who brought them fresh water and a can of vienna sausages. They saw also the prisoners from Santo Tomas prison in Manila, including a woman missionary who had been en route to Peekskill to enter the Novitiate when she was arrested and interned. When they returned to Bilibid they found it had been looted by gangs of Filipino thieves. Their few pitiful possessions had been stolen.

They were cheered, nonetheless, to learn that in a few days they were to go home. General Douglas MacArthur visited Bilibid one morning, and to Sister Columba's surprise, walked over and shook her hand. When he saw the condition of the internees, and even more of the military prisoners, he said grimly, "It has been too long."

By Shrove Tuesday the internees were eating fresh eggs

flown from the United States, and Sister Columba wrote sternly in her diary:

> Henceforth I shall chronicle no more food. We are back to normal with regard to food and are glad to have it play a less important part in our lives. We have been altogether too food conscious.

Their weights had shrunk to eighty-five pounds for Sister Juliana, ninety-seven pounds for Sister Mary Oliva and one-hundred-seven pounds for Sister Columba.

Within a few days they were homeward bound. They were received with much rejoicing by their Sisters in Chicago and in Peekskill. By God's great grace, the Community with its tiny missionary contingent had been permitted to share in some of the tribulations of the War.

The summer passed quickly, the Sisters gained back their strength, and a year after their return they made ready to return to Sagada and set about repairing the ravages of occupation. Sister Columba and Sister Mary Oliva sailed in September, 1946, accompanied by two Sisters going out for the first time. The service of Itinerary, always moving, was made more dramatic by the presence in Choir of the Postulant Marian Electa Davis, whose trip to Peekskill had been interrupted by three years of imprisonment in Santo Tomas.

As the Community approached its one hundredth birthday, Sisters were still at work and prayer in Sagada, though the Christian community in Luzon now had its own bishops, priests and sisters.

215

The Sisters' devotion to St. Mary, their patroness, is usually of the sober and unsentimental variety, reflecting a deeply felt regard for her as mother of all Christians and exemplar of the virtues of faith, love and hidden service. The

GLADYS RICE WASHBURN

Rule requires that the main chapel of every house be dedicated to St. Mary. Statues of her in Community houses vary from simple figures to this ornately carved statue in St. Mary's Chapel, Peekskill, designed by a Sister-artist.

CHAPTER SIXTEEN

Oblation

WITHDRAWAL OF A FREE OBEDIENCE is the fatal ailment of religious communities. By a subtle alchemy the means of obedience become the end, and a hard crust of rigidity encloses and suffocates the life within, resisting formative influences from without. Vigilance is required if communities are to maintain a tough core of principles surrounded by a pliancy which can grow and adapt to the changing needs of the Church and the world.

As its first century closed, the Community of Saint Mary could be grateful that it had somehow eluded this fatal affliction. The early hostility which hastened the Community's development and gave it a tendency toward eclectism should also, it would seem, have encouraged the Sisters to barricade themselves behind a cumbrous institutionalism. That this did not happen stemmed perhaps from the Community spirit, which flowered before the formulations of 1906 and remained to some degree independent of codes; stemmed al-

217

most certainly from the imprint of Mother Harriet, whose cheerfulness, simplicity and self-mortification gave no place to isolation and self-concern; stemmed also from the provincial system, premature as it would seem to have been, which by decentralizing the Community's structure prevented rigidity.

The Community was ready, therefore, to adapt to new work when the changing needs of the twentieth century required new approaches to the Sisters' apostolate. As public welfare agencies assumed responsibility for the poor, the Sisters turned their attention to the needs of the spiritually impoverished. Retreats now became a major work of the Community. Since the early eighties retreats had been provided for Associates and friends. New York newspapers circulated wildly fictitious reports concerning them; society women were depicted in evening dress and then, by way of contrast, in black or grey "retreatants' garb." A snapshot of the faithful old housemaid Ella watering her plants on the porch was published with a caption explaining that she was sprinkling incoming retreatants with holy water. By way of correcting these sensations, Mother Harriet finally gave audience to a reporter of the *New York Sun,* who quoted her denial that the retreat then in progress included socially prominent women, with the Mother's characteristic comment, ". . . as a rule, society people do not care much for the hard work of religion." She added:

> I am sorry to see that some of the papers are trying to make a sensation out of the retreat this year as they did out of the one we held several years ago. A retreat is anything but sensational. It is simply an opportunity for those who take part in it to withdraw from the outside world and escape from their every-

day cares and worries in order that they may spend a little while alone with God, uninterrupted by anyone or anything, in self-examination, prayer and meditation.

It would take years of patient teaching and of small beginnings before the Community could open two full-time retreat centers in the late 1940's. The DeKoven Foundation opened its retreat house on the old Racine College campus, purchased in the depth of the Depression by St. Mary's Home in Chicago as a summer camp for children. Shortly before a pending sheriff's sale on mortgage foreclosure, the Sisters acquired the forty-acre campus overlooking Lake Michigan, thereby saving for the Church the monument and grave-shrine of Dr. James DeKoven. In 1938 the Sisters began year-around occupancy of Taylor Hall and proceeded to the arduous task of restoring the fabric of the splendid old English gothic buildings. The Rev. W. C. R. Sheridan wrote:

> Nothing else quite like DeKoven exists in the American Church. No human being can say how many people it has converted to our Lord Jesus Christ, nor count the number of those whose conversion has been deepened by a visit there. The list of activities is both amazing and endless—and always undergirded and colored by the life of the religious in their daily round of praise.

The guests at DeKoven came to include little girls in leotards dancing on the grass during the camping season, grave seminary students in cassocks in groups of ninety or more, married couples sharing a retreat, and women of the Church holding a provincial meeting, with St. John's Chapel standing serene and sure in the center of the campus, just as it did when James DeKoven's big boys played soccer in its shadow.

St. Mary's Camp, held at DeKoven Foundation every July

and August, came to hold a special place in the hearts of its "alumnae." It was of no small significance to the Community's acceptance in the Midwest that as campers and counsellors, generations of women had lived with and loved the Sisters in an atmosphere of wholesome fun, learning and prayer.

In New York the retreat work grew to such proportions that St. Mary's Hospital on Thirty-fourth Street began scheduling retreats in the Nurses' Training School. When Mrs. Ernesto Fabbri first considered turning over her Italian Renaissance townhouse on Ninety-fifth Street for use as a retreat house, it was to the Sisters at St. Mary's Hospital that she turned. There resulted the House of the Redeemer, and in assuming its management, the Sisters were unwittingly fulfilling an old dream of Mrs. Fabbri's brother-in-law, an artist who had fallen in love with the Church Catholic. He was Egisto Fabbri, who with his brothers Alessandro and Ernesto, was born to an Italian banker and partner in the House of Morgan. After the father's death, Mrs. Fabbri with her three sons and five daughters returned to Florence, where they lived in patriarchal fashion with an uncle. During World War I, Mrs. Edith Shepard Fabbri, wife of Ernesto, cabled Egisto to come to New York and help her plan a quattrocento Italian house. The house he built was like no other in New York. Wrote Mable LaFarge:

> The world of New York was to come and go in it, but even the entrance hall was not New York; it suggested peace, calm, low voices, the beauty of some Brunelleschi sacristy.

Across the front hall, Mrs. LaFarge wrote, were richly panelled walnut doors leading down three steps to the great white-vaulted refectory with red tiled floors and simple massive grey stone fireplace. Wrought-iron candelabra . . . and a few old decorative paintings of Florence. Nothing else to mar the restfulness.

White-vaulted also was the great two-story library with balustraded gallery and magnificent woodwork from a palace in Perugia.

The great house was opened with a dance presenting Mrs. Fabbri's daughter to society. Egisto was a strange dark figure in the gay crowd, muttering miserably to a friend, "But I want to build a chapel." He had heard some nuns in Paris sing Gregorian chant and dreamed of some day restoring the chant to its proper place in the liturgy. His dream came true. He designed and built the Church of the Spirito Santo in Serraville, Italy, and near it a convent for teaching of the chant. He built another such convent on the outskirts of Florence.

Little did Egisto Fabbri guess that the Renaissance town-house he designed for his Episcopalian sister-in-law would one day add a third such foundation to his list. In 1949 Mrs. Fabbri, inspired by a sermon delivered by the Rt. Rev. Austin Pardue, Bishop of Pittsburgh, deeded her home to a corporate organization set up to operate a retreat house. The deed was presented to the president of the corporation, the Rt. Rev. Charles K. Gilbert, Bishop of New York, on November 20, 1949, and nine days later the Sisters began their apostolate there. On February 4, 1950, Bishop Gilbert blessed the chapel, in what had been Mrs. Fabbri's second-floor drawing room. Here, in the room where Egisto Fabbri had glumly watched his niece's guests dancing while he longed to build a chapel, the Sisters now offered their daily round of prayer

221

and praise.

St. Raphael's House, Evergreen, Colorado, operated as a full-time retreat house for six years in the thirties and there-after was opened each summer. Scores of Associates and friends in the western states relied on St. Raphael's for their annual retreat and rest. As the retreat movement spread, Associates initiated and fostered annual retreats in their home dioceses, first in Kansas City, then in Dallas, and eventually in Montana, Oklahoma, Nebraska and New Mexico.

The Community reached out to yet another work in the late forties when the Sisters of the Western Province under-took the management of a parish day school, the Ascension Parish Day School in Sierra Madre, California, near Los Angeles. The Rector, the Rev. Harley G. Smith, opened the school in 1947 with four grades and thirty-five pupils. The enrollment soon grew to eight grades and one hundred pupils, achieving under the Sisters' direction a sound reputation in the field of elementary education.

Less dramatic, but equally important, were advances and improvements in the older schools under the Sisters' direc-tion, advances made possible in countless instances by the loyalty and generosity of devoted alumnae and friends. St. Mary's School, Peekskill, which was formed by combining St. Mary's, New York, with St. Gabriel's, Peekskill, under-took a building program in 1909 which required more than half a century to complete. Ralph Adams Cram designed the splendid collegiate gothic quadrangle which commands a sweeping panorama of the Hudson River Highlands. Pain-stakingly, through the years, by large bequests and small gifts, the building was completed, until in 1963 the swimming pool was added that the Sisters regarded as the final bit of construction. Kemper Hall, with its crowded and inadequate buildings, was preparing at century-end a development program which, it was hoped, would provide facilities to match the school's achievements in the field of preparatory education.

II

An initial assessment of the first century of the Community of Saint Mary would include perforce that it had achieved something merely by surviving. Within two decades, 1852 to 1872, at least eight attempts were made to found Protestant Sisterhoods, in response to a call from the General Convention of 1850. Evangelical leaders required the life of sacrifice divorced from the liturgy of sacrifice, and eight courageous responses were made to this request for fruit without root. Of those eight sisterhoods, only one appears to have survived its founders. By contrast, the Community attempted from the outset to be guided by traditional monastic practice, and prevailed despite ignorance, indifference, hostility and vicissitudes of every kind. The lesson seemed obvious, that in establishing the dedicated communal life it was inadvisable to set aside the considered opinions and established practices of thirteen centuries.

More important than survival was the Community's contribution to the entire process by which the Church in America awakened like an exiled orphan to an awareness of its true identity. Not surprisingly, women played a determining role in the awakening. Eighteenth century rationalism had left its mark on the menfolk, but women's intuitive perception saw past the intellectual roadblocks of deism and dissent to the discipline and worship required or implied by the Book of

Common Prayer, and beyond that to the continuity of the Church in America with Catholic Christendom through the ages. Men sought to trim theology down to fit their finite understanding. The Sisters favored enlarging the human scope to encompass transcendent demands. In 1804 Thomas Jefferson revised the New Testament, expunging references to miracles. To mark the centennial of this triumph, the United States Congress in 1904 published nine thousand facsimile copies of the Jefferson Bible, and not one cry of protest is recorded against this version of separation of Church and State. The religion of this-world, the faith of Almighty Man, had won in the United States. Among the elements of protest was the silent witness of the Sisters of Saint Mary.

More profoundly, the Community left its imprint on the lives of incalculable thousands. Every house acquired a unique character. For example, to generations of nurses, internes, physicians, surgeons, society women and students from the General Seminary who served at the altar, St. Mary's Hospital on Thirty-fourth Street was simply "the Hospital", as if it were the only hospital in the world. Devotees recalled such incidents as the day in 1908 when the trained dogs, monkeys and baby elephant from the Barnum and Bailey Circus came to entertain the wards, the elephant in a grey ulster, snorting and protesting against being taken to a hospital. The be-powdered and be-spangled clowns prepared their act in Sister Catharine's office, she chatting with them as politely as if they were the ladies who called at regular intervals in broughams with liveried coachmen.

Even the geographical extent of the Community's influence could not be fully assessed. Researchists learned not to discount any rumored connection with the Community, however unlikely. The House of Prayer, Newark, New Jersey, claimed to include the Sisters of Saint Mary in its distant past, though the Community archives were silent about the matter. Years later, a chance newspaper article revealed that the indefatigable Sister Amelia had indeed worked two days a week at the House of Prayer in 1875, visiting the poor in connection with a relief store in Plane Street and teaching sewing to girls at the parish industrial school. When Churchmen in Arkansas claimed to have had the services of Sisters in that Diocese, it was found that they referred to a summer camp the Sisters used briefly to protect Church Home orphans from Memphis summers. The Sisters were aware that the Community's influence is always greater than the sum of its parts would indicate, but even that sum was an unknown quantity.

The Guild of Associates in each Province, numbering about ten Associates for every Sister, was important in disseminating the principles of the religious life in many parishes and communities. Many Associates lived lives of heroic and hidden sacrifice and praise, showing forth the Lord's death and resurrection as truly as their Sisters in habits, and putting to the lie the often-made charge that monasticism promotes a duality of "cheap grace and costing grace", to use Bonhoeffer's phrase.

The first century of a religious community comprises its infancy. Perhaps the second century of the Community of Saint Mary would see a further development of the tendencies of the first hundred years, with the Sisters providing for themselves opportunities for greater enclosure and contemplative prayer, and assisting by prayer and encouragement their Associate Sisters who bear Christ into office and factory, classroom and hospital, home and studio. With a splendid vision, Mother Mary Maude suggested this as far back as 1934 when she wrote that religious houses have always served as "conservators of the ascetic ideal . . . schools and universities in relation to the rest of the world." She wrote:

> It has been said that this age is ripe for a new manifestation in the monastic tradition. There has been no distinctively new note of development since the Jesuit ideals entered the stream of tradition. One wonders in what way it will come. Perhaps in lay organizations, pledged to the ascetic ideal, yet living and mingling in the world. If ever the world needed the salt of distinctively Christian lives it needs it now. Such lives must be based on the theological virtues, built up on the moral virtues, pledged to simple and frugal living, detached from worldly standards, fired with a passion for social justice, and sustained by a dynamic energy drawn from sacramental grace and nourished by a systematic prayer life.

Whatever the second century might hold, the Sisters could be certain that God would provide opportunity for a full oblation of themselves. They could be grateful for the noble precedents of the first century and for the lessons provided by faults and failings. And they could sum up their Sisters' achievements by saying simply that a few women went forth in faith into wastelands of the human spirit, and that the desert blossomed like the rose.

226

Notes and Sources

CHAPTER ONE

Ayres, Anne, THE LIFE AND WORK OF WILLIAM AUGUSTUS MUHLENBERG. New York, Thomas Whittaker. 1889.

Billington, Ray Allen, THE PROTESTANT CRUSADE, 1800-1860. A STUDY OF THE ORIGINS OF AMERICAN NATIVISM. New York, Macmillan. 1938.

Johnson, Allen and Malone, Dumas, (eds.), DICTIONARY OF AMERICAN BIOGRAPHY. New York, Scribner's Sons. 1930.

Muhlenberg, William Augustus, (ed.), THE TRUE MARY. BEING MRS. BROWNING'S POEM "THE VIRGIN MARY TO THE CHILD JESUS" WITH COMMENTS AND NOTES. New York, Thomas Whittaker. 1871. (Designated as the work of one of the Sisters of Saint Luke's Hospital.)

Newton, William Wilberforce, DR. MUHLENBERG. New York, Houghton, Mifflin. 1890.

[No Author] AWFUL EXPOSURE OF THE ATROCIOUS PLOT FORMED BY CERTAIN INDIVIDUALS AGAINST THE CLERGY AND NUNS OF LOWER CANADA THROUGH THE INTERVENTION OF MARIA MONK (with an authentic narrative of her life from her birth to the present moment, and an account of her impositions, etc.). New York, Printed for Jones & Co. of Montreal. 1836.

Sister Hilary, C.S.M., A STUDY IN THE ANGLICAN REVIVAL OF THE RELIGIOUS LIFE IN THE NINETEENTH CENTURY, BEING THE LIFE OF HARRIET STARR CANNON, MOTHER FOUNDRESS OF THE FIRST AMERICAN COMMUNITY. Unpublished ms. in the archives of the Community of Saint Mary.

Skardon, Alvin Wilson, WILLIAM A. MUHLENBERG: PIONEER URBAN CHURCH LEADER. Department of Photoduplication, University of Chicago Library. 1960. Thesis, University of Chicago.

Van Rensselaer, M., SISTER LOUISE. THE STORY OF HER LIFE AND WORK. New York, Young. 1883.

White, Charles I., LIFE OF MRS. ELIZA A. SETON, FOUNDRESS AND FIRST SUPERIOR OF THE SISTERS OR DAUGHTERS OF CHARITY. Baltimore, Kelly, Piet. 1879.

The Churchman, January 23, 1875, carried an account of the reception of Sister Annette into the "Memorial Sisterhood" to work as a nurse in the

Cottage Hospital and as a parish visitor of Gethsemane Church in Minneapolis. The ceremony was held at the Bishop Potter Memorial House in Philadelphia, with Bishop Whipple acting for the Bishop of Pennsylvania.

American Journal of Nursing, December, 1929. pp. 1466 to 1484. An interesting account of the contribution of Anglican Sisters to the development of the nursing profession in the United States.

The American Church Review of July, 1862, quoted the Second Annual Report of St. Luke's Hospital to the effect that the Sisterhood of the Holy Communion "strongly resembles the Institution of the Lutheran Deaconesses at Kaiserswerth. Though the former was not copied from the latter, and was formed with scarcely any knowledge of it, the two in their spirit and principle are remarkably the same. . ."

Unidentified clipping in the archives of the Community: "Sister Frances of St. Johnland, Kings Park, N.Y., died on Oct. 15, 1940, the last surviving member of the first American Sisterhood, the Sisters of the Holy Communion. Born Eva Frances Lucas in Winchester, England in 1864, she came to Canada as a child. She was graduated from Boston City College Nursing School in 1892 and joined the Sisterhood of the Holy Communion in 1897. . . Sister Frances, because of her solitary state and nature of her work, led a more secular life than the Sisters in New York. She was criticized for this and offered to resign from the Order. Dr. Mottet, Rector of the Church of the Holy Communion, refused to accept her resignation. . . . In 1920 she suffered a breakdown in health and was forced to give up her work. She continued to live at St. Johnland until her death. She was buried in St. Johnland Cemetery, at the foot of Dr. Muhlenberg's grave."

CHAPTER TWO

Brand, William Francis, LIFE OF WILLIAM ROLLINSON WHITTINGHAM. 2 vols. New York, Young. 1883.

Peters, John Punnett, ANNALS OF ST. MICHAEL'S. New York, G. P. Putnam's Sons. 1907.

Sister Teresa, C.S.M., ANNALS. Unpublished manuscript memoirs of Sister Teresa, number nine in order of profession, professed in 1871, died in 1874.

CHAPTER THREE

Hodges, George, HENRY CODMAN POTTER, SEVENTH BISHOP OF NEW YORK. New York, Macmillan. 1915.

Hooper, Joseph, A HISTORY OF ST. PETER'S CHURCH IN THE CITY OF ALBANY. Albany, Ft. Orange Press. 1900.

Howe, Mark Anthony DeWolfe, MEMOIRS OF THE LIFE AND SERVICES OF THE RT. REV. ALONZO POTTER. Philadelphia, Lippincott. 1871.

Potter, Frank Hunter, THE ALONZO POTTER FAMILY. Privately printed. 1923.

——————————, THE POTTER RECORD. Privately printed. 1921.

Potter, Henry Codman, SISTERHOODS AND DEACONESSES. New York, Dutton. 1873.

Unpublished manuscript letters, archives of the Community of Saint Mary.

Wilson, James Grant (ed.), THE CENTENNIAL HISTORY OF THE PROT-ESTANT EPISCOPAL CHURCH IN THE DIOCESE OF NEW YORK 1785-1885. New York, D. Appleton. 1886.

> The Brother Bishops, Alonzo Potter and Horatio Potter, held diverse views regarding women's vocation to the religious life. Dr. Howe identifies Bishop Alonzo Potter as the man who in 1850 introduced a measure in the House of Bishops calling for revival of the order of Deaconesses. "He did not contemplate the creation of permanent com-munities, bound under conventual vows to celibacy, and lifelong pur-suit of some line of duty. He did not wish to call romantic young girls away from their homes, and by the fascination of peculiar vestments and the ceremonious conferring of successive veils imbue them with the conceit that so they might attain a peculiar sanctity." p. 334.

CHAPTER FOUR

City Mission Society, *Sixteenth Annual Report.* 1866.

City Mission Society, *Seventeenth Annual Report.* 1867.

City Mission Work Leaflet II, December, 1865.

City Mission Work Leaflet V, February, 1867.

Dix, Morgan, BOOK OF HOURS. New York, Hurd & Houghton. 1866.

CHAPTER FIVE

Dix, Morgan, Microfilmed diary. *Archives of Trinity Church, New York.*

House of Mercy, *Seventh Annual Report.* 1866.

Muhlenberg, William Augustus, THE WOMAN AND HER ACCUSERS, A PLEA FOR THE MIDNIGHT MISSION. New York, Pliny F. Smith. 1870.

Richmond, John Francis, NEW YORK AND ITS INSTITUTIONS, 1609-1872. New York, E. B. Treat. 1872.

Roche, Olin Scott, FORTY YEARS OF PARISH LIFE AND WORK, 1883-1923. (St. Peter's Chelsea.) New York, Friebelle Press. 1930.

Sister Gertrude, *unpublished manuscript memoirs,* dictated in 1914.

Williams, Thomas J., ANGLICAN VERSIONS OF THE BREVIARY. Reprinted from Cowley, July, 1955.

Dr. Roche wrote that the connection of the Sisterhood of the Good Shepherd with St. Barnabas House was severed in 1886 when the Sisterhood moved to a rented house in Ninth Avenue between 21st and 22nd Streets. Soon after, the Sisters purchased 417 and 419 West 19th Street. Sister Adelia was the head of the House, directing work among the poor and at St. Peter's parish, and a Seaside Home at Asbury Park, N.J. The Sisters worked in St. Peter's, Chelsea, until about 1900. pp. 148-149.

CHAPTER SIX

The newspaper clippings which comprise the chief source for this chapter are preserved in scrapbooks in the archives of the Community, undated in most cases, and imperfectly identified in some.

CHAPTER SEVEN

Church Journal, July 2, 1874.

Churchman, July 7, 1875.

Commercial Advertiser, (n.d.), 1875 and November 23, 1877.

Harper's Weekly, February 9, 1878.

New York News, (n.d.), 1881. Among the benefactions listed were sixty toy trumpets.

New York Times, February 23, 1876.

Rae, Gwynedd, LOVELY HERITAGE. Bedford, Sydney Press. 1962. This biographical sketch of the author's mother and aunt includes allusions to their days at St. Mary's School in Manhattan: ". . . inside was the inevitable confinement of a city school, with its rules and regulations . . . but the Sisters of St. Mary were sweet to the children and soon won their hearts and trust and, to the end of their lives, 'Mother Harriet' and 'Sister Catherine' (sic) were held in deepest affection."

Entries in Dr. Dix's diary indicate that the Guild of the Holy Child, still extant and vigorous at Kemper Hall and at Sagada, admitted its first members on November 27, 1871. Initially, this Guild was for the younger children at St. Mary's School. St. Hilda's Guild, for older students, admitted eleven charter members on June 21, 1871.

CHAPTER EIGHT

Davis, John H. ST. MARY'S CATHEDRAL, 1858-1958. Memphis, The Chapter of St. Mary's Cathedral (Gailor Memorial). 1958.

Gailor, Thomas Frank, SOME MEMORIES. Kingsport, Tennessee, Southern Publishers. 1937.

Noll, Arthur Howard (ed.), DOCTOR QUINTARD. Sewanee, University Press. 1905.

Noll, Arthur Howard (ed.), HISTORY OF THE CHURCH IN THE DIOCESE OF TENNESSEE. New York, James Pott. 1900.

[No Author] THE SISTERS OF ST. MARY AT MEMPHIS. New York, printed but not published. 1879. Morgan Dix edited this collection of letters, which includes valuable accounts of the priests involved in the epidemic of 1878.

> Dr. Davis includes the curious story that the parish of which Charles Parsons was originally rector had been founded in 1865 and was dedicated to St. Lazarus "because he was licked by dogs." After Parson's heroic death, the combined parish of Grace and St. Lazarus became Grace Church.

> Annual Reports of the Church Home include lists of contributions, such as these from the report of 1873-1874:
> "1 bucket of country butter."
> "1 coop of chickens from two colored men at Bradley's Landing."
> "Creed Taylor, Esq. . . . bale of cotton, $500."

CHAPTER NINE

Burial Registry, St. Mary's Cathedral, Memphis.

[No Author] THE SISTERS OF ST. MARY AT MEMPHIS. New York, printed but not published. 1879.

Dromgoole, J. P., YELLOW FEVER HEROES, HONORS AND HORRORS OF 1878. Louisville, John P. Morton. 1879.

Gailor, Thomas Frank, SOME MEMORIES. Kingsport, Tennessee, Southern Publishers. 1937.

Harris, George C, THE MEMORIAL SERMON PREACHED IN ST. MARY'S CATHEDRAL, MEMPHIS, DECEMBER 22, 1878. New York, Bedell & Brother.

Joyce, John Jay, A SERMON PREACHED UPON THE OCCASION OF THE EUCHARISTIC COMMEMORATION OF THE CLERGY AND SISTERS WHO FELL VICTIMS TO THE FEVER IN THE SOUTH. St. John's Church, Washington, D.C. Feast of All Saints. Washington, Beresford. 1878.

Keating, J. M., THE YELLOW FEVER EPIDEMIC. Memphis, Howard Association. 1879.

Memphis Commercial-Appeal, September 30, 1962.

[No Editor] A MEMORIAL OF LOUIS SANDFORD SCHUYLER, PRIEST. New York, Pott, Young. 1879. (J. E. Learned, Rector of the House of Prayer in Newark, provided the preface.)

Quintard, Charles Todd. IN MEMORIAM, THE REV. CHARLES CARROLL PARSONS, RECTOR OF GRACE CHURCH, MEMPHIS. A SERMON PREACHED BEFORE THE NASHVILLE CONVOCATION, IN GRACE CHAPEL, SPRING HILL, TENN. New York, E. P. Dutton. 1879.

Tennessee State Board of Health, First Report, April 1877 to October 1878. Nashville, Tavel & Howell, 1880.

Dr. White, the Rector of Calvary Church, whose name rarely appears in stories of the 1878 epidemic, did nevertheless remain in the city and ministered to the dying and bereaved insofar as his health permitted. Bishop Gailor wrote that Dr. White would go to the cemetery early in the morning and remain there all day, officiating at one burial after another.

Dr. Gailor related that in the exodus from Memphis one of the steamboats, the "Golden Crown", was stranded at Paducah when yellow fever broke out on board; people on shore lined the river bank with guns to prevent the packet from landing.

CHAPTER TEN

Birdsall, Ralph, THE STORY OF COOPERSTOWN. Cooperstown, Crist.

Community of Saint Mary. *Chapter Minutes in the General Archives.*

DeKoven, James, *Typescript of Journal, Volume II.*

Dix, Morgan, HARRIET STARR CANNON, FIRST MOTHER SUPERIOR OF THE SISTERHOOD OF ST. MARY. New York, Longmans. 1896. Dr. Dix described this as a "brief memoir" and it is scarcely more than that.

Hughson, S. C., HARRIET STARR CANNON AND THE FUNDAMENTAL IDEALS OF THE COMMUNITY OF SAINT MARY. (An address to the associates of the community by the Rev. S. C. Hughson, O.H.C., Chaplain General, Advent, 1915.) Privately printed. Peekskill, St. Mary's Convent.

Manuscript letters, newspaper clippings and notes.

Sister Hilary, C.S.M., THE LIFE OF HARRIET STARR CANNON ETC. Unpublished manuscript. This massive and painstaking work was an invaluable source.

[No Author] A MEMOIR OF THE LIFE AND WORK OF HANNAH GRIER COOME, MOTHER-FOUNDRESS OF THE SISTERHOOD OF ST. JOHN THE DIVINE. London, Oxford Press. 1933.

Powers, Louise Brooks, ST. MARY'S HOME. (A dissertation submitted to the faculty of the School of Social Service Administration, University of Chicago, in candidacy for the degree of Master of Arts.) Typescript.

CHAPTERS ELEVEN AND TWELVE

Community of Saint Mary, *Chapter Minutes in the General Archives.*

Hawks, Edward, WILLIAM MCGARVEY AND THE OPEN PULPIT, AN INTIMATE HISTORY OF A CELIBATE MOVEMENT IN THE EPISCOPAL CHURCH AND OF ITS COLLAPSE, 1870-1908. Philadelphia, Dolphin Press. 1935.

Hayward, William L., THE C.S.S.S., THE QUEST AND GOAL OF THE FOUNDER. Philadelphia, Jeffries & Manz. 1940.

Sister Mary Theodora, C.S.M., A MEMORABLE DECADE, 1898-1908. *Manuscript in the General Archives.*

Both the Hayward and Hawks accounts suffer from inaccuracies and inadequate sources, but they provide fascinating glimpses of the Companions' ultramontanism. Father Hawks refers to a visit to Nashotah of "the Rev. Wilfred (sic) Douglas" with this exclamation, "Douglas, who was an authority of plain chant, and our visiting instructor in regard to it, seriously discussed the possibility of Mass in English being permitted by the Pope!"

CHAPTERS THIRTEEN AND FOURTEEN

Extensive source material in the archives of the Eastern Province at Peekskill, including memoirs of the three Sisters interned, a splendid account assembled by Sister Mary Maude, and letters.

CHAPTERS FIFTEEN AND SIXTEEN

Letters and minutes of Chapter meetings.

Mothers Superior, Community of Saint Mary

Mothers General